# White House Sermons

# White House Sermons

## Introduction by
## President Richard Nixon

Edited by
### BEN HIBBS

1817
HARPER & ROW, PUBLISHERS
New York • Evanston • San Francisco • London

BV
4241
.H5

Grateful acknowledgment is made to the following publishers for permission
to reprint copyrighted material:
Branden Press, Inc. for the lines from "The Book" from *Garment of Praise* by
Helen Frazee-Bower.
Moody Press for "God's Hall of Fame" from *Homespun Poems* by Walt Huntley.
Copyright © 1969. Moody Press, Moody Bible Institute of Chicago.
Vantage Press, Inc. for "A Mother Speaks" from *Bluegrass Seasons* by Alice
Kennelly Roberts. Copyright © 1960 by Alice Kennelly Roberts.

WHITE HOUSE SERMONS. Copyright © 1972 by Harper & Row, Inc. All rights
reserved. Printed in the United States of America. No part of this book may be
used or reproduced in any manner whatsoever without written permission except
in the case of brief quotations embodied in critical articles and reviews. For
information address Harper & Row, Publishers, Inc., 49 East 33rd Street, New
York, N.Y. 10016. Published simultaneously in Canada by Fitzhenry & Whiteside
Limited, Toronto.

FIRST EDITION

LIBRARY OF CONGRESS CATALOG CARD NUMBER: 70-184407

Designed by C. Linda Dingler

# Introduction by
# President Richard Nixon

It was Sunday morning, January 26, 1969. Just six days earlier I had taken the oath of office as President of the United States, and on that Sunday I was attempting to inaugurate what I hoped would become a White House institution.

Outside, on the White House grounds and in the adjacent parks, the trees stood bare against 'the winter sky—a reminder, perhaps, of the critical problems confronting this nation. But inside, in the historic East Room, there was an air of warmth— a warmth of spirit engendered by human friendliness, faith in God and country, and the magnetism of one of the most remarkable preachers of our time. My long-time friend Billy Graham was speaking to a congregation of some two hundred persons whom Mrs. Nixon and I had invited to this first Sunday Worship Service in the White House.

Many of those present in that first congregation, and in those that followed, were from the ranks of government—Senators and Congressmen, Supreme Court justices, members of the Diplomatic Corps, White House staff people, Cabinet members fresh in their new jobs, with their wives and children. Others were simply friends whom Mrs. Nixon and I thought might enjoy "going to church" with their families in a new and different setting.

That expression "going to church" calls to mind a criticism which inevitably has been leveled from time to time at our Sunday

Worship Services. Some persons have said that I was wrong in holding religious services in a hall or room which was not consecrated wholly to the Lord's work but was used for secular purposes, including occasional social events.

Actually, this practice accords with the history of religion and its practice down through the years. Since the beginning of group religious services way back in early human history, men have worshiped God wherever they could. In our own pioneer days— particularly during the settlement of the West—services were often held in country schoolhouses, in people's homes, in barns and carriage houses, in lodge halls and other secular meeting places. I feel that it is entirely in order to convert the great East Room—which has seen the making of so much American history —into a "church" on Sunday mornings. It serves as an appropriate reminder that we feel God's presence here, and that we seek His guidance here—and that ours is, in the words of the Pledge of Allegiance, "one nation, under God, indivisible. . . ."

I grew up in a home where religion was an important ingredient of our lives. We went to church as a matter of course, as did most of our friends and acquaintances. It was an era when people, generally speaking, took their religious commitments more seriously than many people do now.

Americans still are basically a religious people, but under the pressures of modern life it often seems that religious observances are subordinated to other pursuits.

When I was elected to the highest office in the land, I decided that I wanted to do something to encourage attendance at services and to emphasize this country's basic faith in a Supreme Being. It seemed to me that one way of achieving this was to set a good example. What better example could there be than to bring the worship service, with all its solemn meaning, right into the White House? I talked with a number of ministers whom I knew, and they were enthusiastic. To be sure, most of our Presidents have attended church more or less regularly—but so far as our White House historians can determine, regular worship services had never before been held in the Executive Mansion.

Another compelling reason why I wanted to have services in the White House was my intense dislike of "going to church for show." In my family, worship was always a very private matter. Whenever a President goes out to church, the news media—quite understandably—feel obligated to cover it, with the result that batteries of still and television news cameras follow him. This is not my idea of the atmosphere that should surround a worship service.

In my inaugural address, I had said: "To a crisis of the spirit, we need an answer of the spirit." This was and is a matter about which I feel deeply. And so on the first Sunday after my inauguration, we held our initial Sunday Worship Service in the White House.

I wish we could throw open the doors to all who wish to attend these services, but because the East Room can accommodate only a very limited congregation—the maximum is about three hundred—attendance must be by invitation. Symbolically, however, I have regarded our White House services as a standing invitation to all men and women of good will to participate—in their own place and their own way—in the "answer of the spirit" which this nation so urgently needs.

To avoid any suggestion of favoritism, we have chosen ministers of various faiths and from different regions of this country. Catholics, Jews, and most of the major Protestant denominations have been represented. Our "White House preachers" have come from the East and West Coasts, the Middle West and the South. We have even had a wide range in age brackets. Several of the ministers have been outstanding younger men. An occasional youthful viewpoint in matters of the spirit, we felt, might enlighten and nourish the souls of some of us who were more mature.

Although I always make the final choice of the minister for each

Worship Service, I do have some good help—for which I am most grateful. Some of the ministers have been old friends of mine, or persons whom I had heard preach elsewhere, whom I admired and wanted for our White House services. In addition, Cabinet members, Congressmen, White House staffers, and other friends often recommend their favorite ministers, or ones who they feel would be especially appropriate. My daily mail yields many nominations. Occasionally, a clergyman writes me to offer his own services.

In my opinion, all of our White House sermons have been good and some of them outstanding. Most have been relevant to the time and the place—thoughtful, socially conscious, warmly human, and deeply reverent. We have been truly honored by the presence of these devout and talented men, and I think most of them have felt honored to be at the White House.

We also have been most fortunate in the singing groups we have been able to assemble. Many choirs, college choral organizations, and other musical groups have appeared at the White House. Some of them have been on tour, and it was our good luck that they were able to fit our Sunday Worship Services into their already heavy schedules.

In arranging our programs, we have purposely avoided any attempt to place these choirs and choral groups in services conducted by a person representing their own faith or denomination. We believe in the ecumenical principle, and if it turns out that a Methodist choir sings at a service conducted by a Cardinal of the Catholic Church, we feel it may contribute to the broadening of religious thinking and practice in this beloved America of ours.

We of course have not been able to schedule a White House Worship Service every Sunday morning. However, during the first two years of my administration, 1969 and 1970, we were able to hold White House Worship Services twenty-six times. Three of these were Christmas programs—two of them in 1969 and one in 1970—composed entirely of music and Scriptural readings. So during those two years there were twenty-three White House sermons. These were all recorded as they were given. Later the tapes were transcribed, and the transcriptions were edited to provide the manuscript for this book. I am proud that the White House sermons are now in this permanent form, and I hope that there will be other volumes like this one during the coming years.

It is my intention to continue the Sunday Worship Services as long as I remain in the White House. I think they mean a great deal to many people. I know they do to me.

Richard Nixon

# Contents

# White House Sermons

# January 26, 1969

Prelude

Opening Remarks          THE PRESIDENT

Doxology
> *Praise God, from whom all blessings flow;*
> *Praise Him, all creatures here below;*
> *Praise Him above, ye heav'nly host:*
> *Praise Father, Son, and Holy Ghost!*

Prayer          THE REVEREND DR. BILLY GRAHAM

Hymn          *"All Hail the Power"*

Solo          MR. GEORGE BEVERLY SHEA
*"How Great Thou Art"*

Sermon

Benediction

Postlude

# The Reverend Dr. Billy Graham

THE PRESIDENT: Mrs. Nixon and I want to extend a very warm welcome to all of those who have come to attend this first Worship Service in the East Room of the White House. Conducting the service this morning is a long-time personal friend, who, incidentally, will be leaving shortly for Australia to conduct a series of services in that country—Billy Graham.

DR. GRAHAM: Our Father and our God, we come into thy presence this morning in the name of Jesus Christ our Lord, thanking thee and praising thee for all the blessings that thou hast given to us as a people, both spiritual and material. We thank thee for this house and all that it stands for in the history of this nation. We thank thee that we are a nation under God and that our forefathers handed us this torch of faith. And we thank thee that on this Lord's Day, along with millions of Americans who are in churches throughout the nation, we are honoring thee and worshiping thee as the only true God in sovereign law. And we pray that thy blessings shall be upon this service and that each of us will be conscious of thy presence. We pray especially for the President and his family, the Vice President and his family, the members of the Cabinet and their families, that thou wouldst lead and direct and bless them, and may they have a strength and a wisdom that is beyond their own. For we ask it in the name of Jesus Christ our Lord. Amen.

Mr. President, Mrs. Nixon, Mr. Vice President, Mrs. Agnew, distinguished guests: Naturally it is a great privilege for me to be

1

here on the occasion of the first service held in this room during the current administration.

The last time I was at church with the President was about three or four weeks ago today, and I noticed during the early part of the service he became a little bit nervous about something, and he leaned over to me just before the collection was taken and said, "I have no money with me." Then he added, "Could you lend me some money?" And so I loaned him the biggest bill that I had, and I noticed this morning that no collection is listed in the order of service.

I remember that when I first used to be introduced to speak, I was introduced—and have been through the years—as an evangelist. And I used to have to apologize for that, because we came through the Elmer Gantry era and people wondered what an evangelist was. The word "evangelist" comes from the Greek and means "a proclaimer." All the Apostles were called evangelists. We think of St. John, the Evangelist, St. Mark, the Evangelist. The word evangelist is a great term. Many people don't realize that some of our great universities like Princeton and Dartmouth were founded by evangelists.

As a matter of fact, the British Labour Party was founded by an evangelist. An evangelist from America by the name of D. L. Moody was preaching in Great Britain before the turn of the century. A young fellow was converted to Christ and came to Mr. Moody and said, "What can I do for God?" And Mr. Moody said, "Help the laboring people of Scotland." That man, whose name was Keir Hardie, became an evangelist, but he also founded the British Labour Party.

Evangelists have thus had quite an important role, both socially and in the church, through the years. I'm glad to say that we have lived to see the day in America when all denominations now have evangelists who go out preaching and proclaiming the message.

Today I want to take the background for what I have to say in my sermon from President Nixon's inaugural address. He made this statement: "To a crisis of the spirit, we need an answer of the spirit." I don't think I've ever read a passage that so pinpoints the problems of our generation in America and throughout the world as that statement—"a crisis of the spirit." I want also to take us back many hundreds of years to a man that went through a crisis of the spirit and finally found fulfillment—and an answer to the problems and the questions of his generation. His name was Solomon.

Many people ask me if there are any lasting effects in my talks? Sometimes I answer by telling them about an airplane ride I was on about two years ago. I was going from New York to Charlotte, North Carolina, and there was a big fat man on board the plane —and he was drunk. He was flirting with the stewardess and making himself obnoxious to everybody around, cursing, swearing. When we got airborne, he decided to go help the pilot fly the plane. And the copilot had to bring him back and put him in his seat. And somebody across the aisle whispered to him that I was sitting behind him. He got up again and in front of everybody he said, "You don't say." He said to me, "Are you Billy Graham?" And I meekly admitted I was. He said, "Put her there." Then he added, "Your sermons have sure helped me." So I don't know whether my sermon today will have a lasting effect, but I suspect that because of where it is and under the circumstances, it may be remembered.

But let us return to Solomon, who was the King of Israel when Israel was at the peak of her power. Solomon made this statement. He said, "I'm going to try all the experiences of life. I'm going to have all the pleasures, all that money can give me, and then I'm going to tell you the result at the end of it." And at the end of his life, after he'd lived through this fantastic life, he said, "Vanity of vanities, all is vanity." He wrote an entire Book in the Bible called *Ecclesiastes* dealing with his experiences. The Bible gives a lot of descriptions of Solomon. More time is given to Solomon than any other king in the Bible. At the end of it,

Solomon said in effect that he had lived through it all and it wasn't worth it.

I want us to see some of the things that the Bible says about Solomon.

First of all, it is said that he had the greatest knowledge of any man, not only of his generation, but of any man that ever lived except one—and that one was Christ. He said in Ecclesiastes 1, "I've got more wisdom than all they that have been before me or those that will follow after me." He not only had knowledge, but he had wisdom, because in his prayer to God upon his ascension to the throne, he prayed for wisdom and God gave him extraordinary wisdom. And then he said this: "I gave my heart to know wisdom, and I perceive that this also is vexation of spirit, for in much knowledge is much grief." Vanity of vanities. He tried to find the answer to the riddles and the puzzles of life in wisdom and in knowledge, and he didn't find it. That's the reason that today our most educated people are still searching. A few months ago one of the greatest mathematicians in this country asked to see me. He sat in my hotel room, and he said, "If I don't find an answer to the purpose and the reason of my existence, I'm going to commit suicide." He added, "My family life is a mess, my own life is a mess." He said, "I'm already on drugs seeking an escape." Here's a man who is known all over the world for his great knowledge of mathematics, but something was missing down inside.

The Queen of Sheba came to see Solomon, and after she had sat at his feet for awhile, she said, "The half has not been told." Yet Solomon said, "I don't find life's satisfaction in knowledge and wisdom." And this is what the Bible says. The Bible says you cannot find God through wisdom and through knowledge. You could search for God all your life and be the most brilliant man in the world and still not find God because the Bible says, in Second Corinthians, that our minds have been affected by sin. The Bible says all of us are born with a tendency toward sin, toward evil. We may keep it under control so that we don't become criminals, but the Bible says that all of us have the tendency toward lust and greed and lying and selfishness, and we try to escape through great education.

The night before last, I was sitting beside the Governor of Illinois at a banquet in Chicago and he said, "You know, I ran my campaign on education. We're going to do everything we can to increase the facilities and the opportunities of education in the State of Illinois." And I said to the Governor, "That is fine. I think that's a great program and I think you're right." But then I added, "In our education in America, we must remember that man is a trinity. He's a mind that needs educating, he's a body that needs physical exercise and athletics and medicine, but he's also a spirit. And the crisis of America today is the crisis of the spirit."

The Bible says, "The god of this world hath blinded the minds of them which believe not." Sin has affected our minds. It has affected our intellectual processes so that through the intellect alone we cannot find God. Then how do you find God? You find God by faith, simple childlike faith. That's the reason that a little washerwoman back in the mountains of North Carolina where I live can know God. She's never seen the inside of a college. She's never been to high school. But she has a simple faith. And she has answers to some of the problems of life that the professors at the university don't have—because *there is* a simple childlike faith in God.

Secondly, Solomon gave himself to pleasure. He said in Ecclesisastes 2:1, "I have said in my heart I shall prove thee with mirth, therefore enjoy pleasure." He really had pleasure. Now, there's a lovely swimming pool here at the White House, but you ought to read about his swimming pool. It was flanked by twelve lions of gleaming bronze, and the Bible says it dazzled the eyes of all who beheld it. He drank the finest wines from golden goblets. He had seven hundred wives and three hundred concubines. Talk about sex, pleasure, sensual pleasure. He had it all. With every imaginable device of pleasure and lust at his fingertips, Solomon sat out under the stars one night and contemplated it all, and he said it's not worth it—that he hadn't found happiness and peace in all these pleasures at his disposal.

And this is what Job said: "Though wickedness be sweet in your mouth, though you hide it under your tongue, yet there'll come a time when you'll want to spit it out." The Bible says, "But she that liveth in pleasure is dead while she liveth." You see, you can have pleasure for the body, and the soul can be empty and sick. This is exactly, I think, what is happening to many of our people, because we have an affluent society. Some of the most unhappy people are not all in the ghettos. Some of the unhappiest people are in the suburbs. Why? Because we've been trying to get pleasure through materialism alone, and it won't work. It must come from the heart and from the spirit, because the Bible says, "In thy presence is fullness of joy."

The happiest people I know are people that know God. They have the biggest time. They have the heartiest laugh. Sometimes I go into a hotel late at night, and people are having parties, and I listen to their laughter. It's so different from the laughter of some people I've perhaps just come from who have a strong faith in God. Real fun and joy and assurance come in knowing God.

Thirdly, Solomon was the richest man in the history of the world, probably. I haven't figured it out. Secretary Kennedy might be able to take the figures that are given and figure it all out for us. In any event, Solomon's income was staggering. The Bible says "the weight of gold that came to Solomon in one year was six hundred threescore and six talents of gold." I figure that each talent was worth about $25,000 in that day before inflation, and so his take-home pay was about $16,500,000 a year. That was besides all the expenses. And listen to his grocery bill: Two hundred and eighty-one bushels of fine flour every day. Five hundred and sixty-six bushels of meal. Ten fat oxen out of an ox stall. A hundred sheep besides the deer and the fowl. That was his daily grocery bill at the palace.

But one night he sat on the roof of his country home in Lebanon—one of the finest country estates in the world, of any generation—and he had indigestion. He clutched his empty heart and he said, "Vanity of vanities." He added to himself, "All this money that I have, all this wealth that I have, hasn't satisfied something deep inside of me."

The Bible says, "A little that a righteous man hath is better than the riches of many wicked." Jesus said, "For a man's life consists not in the abundance of the things that he has." How true that is! I was on an island in the Caribbean some time ago, and I was invited to visit the home of a very wealthy man. He was seventy-five years of age, and he spent the entire time telling me how miserable he was. We went into his study afterward and had a prayer together. I left his home and went down on a beach, and there was a little old Baptist pastor that came to see me. He, too, was seventy-five. He had two invalid sisters that he took care of at his home. He had no help. He made three dollars a week from his little congregation. He jumped around, happy as a lark, and he said, "I'm the happiest man on this island." That evening as I sat out under the stars on that little island I thought to myself, who was the richest? "A little that a righteous man hath is better than the riches of many wicked."

Fourthly, Solomon had great power. Nobody dared attack Solomon when he was King of Israel. It was the only time in Israel's history when Israel was the greatest power in the world. He had the greatest navy, the greatest army, the greatest power in the world. He never had a war because they were afraid to attack when Solomon was King. But he said this didn't bring him happiness.

Then he tried the aesthetic life. He developed a love for art and music and culture. He said, "I looked upon all the works of my hands and on the labor that I had labored to do, and beheld all the vanity and vexation of spirit and there was no profit under the sun." He said all the concerts he went to and all the art treasures he collected didn't bring him the peace he was looking for.

Lastly, he tried religion. But it's a very strange thing that he didn't find peace in religion either. He tried it in the wrong direction. He built a great temple, the most beautiful temple the world has ever known. It took seven years to build, a hundred thousand men to build it.

There's a great search in this country for peace and security and joy and happiness. And I think the hippies are saying something to us. I like their little motto: "Tune in and turn on and drop out." You see, they wear their hair long and they have their beards and they wear their boots and they call them "Jesus boots." I have talked to a lot of these hippies. I went to the places where they live, and then one night I put on a baseball cap and dark glasses and went to a love-in in Winnipeg—attended by three thousand of them. I had an education that night, I can assure you. They didn't know who I was and I learned a lot. One thing I learned: They were searching for something.

Last summer Sargent Shriver, our Ambassador to Paris, asked me if I would come to his home in Paris and meet some of the student leaders in France and talk to them. He said, "I think it will be an interesting evening." I said, "I will," and I flew over to see him. That evening we met with some of these student leaders, and we had several hours of discussion. When it was over, both he and I agreed that the thing these French students were searching for was something spiritual. The questions they were asking were really theological questions.

And this is what the young people today are screaming about on the campus. They may not know it. They may not articulate it. We know there's a hard core of anarchists, but there's also a great group of young people today who are asking spiritual questions, and they're saying that the system is not answering these questions they're asking. There's a "crisis of the spirit" there on the campus.

But there is an answer, because after Solomon tried religion, he found the answer in a true experience with God, because he said in the very end, "Remember now thy Creator in the days of thy youth, while the evil days come not, nor the years draw nigh." He advised all the people following him, all the people who were trying to climb to the top where he was. He said, "Remember your Creator. What I have not found in any of these other directions, I've found in a personal experience with God."

You can go to church all your life—and I know thousands of people who go to church, but they haven't found fulfillment. They haven't found the peace that they've been looking for. They haven't found the answer to their own deep personal needs. They haven't found it in the church. But you can find it in a personal relationship with God. And this is what Christianity is all about, an existential experience, an experience in which I can know God for myself. This is what Christ said. He said, "You must be born again." He said, "You have to become like a little child and be converted."

Now let's examine the word "conversion." We carry with it the idea of emotion. It's not emotion at all. It simply means to change. I've changed my attitude toward God, changed my attitude toward myself and recognized my dependency upon Him. This is why we have Good Friday and Easter. Christ came and died on the cross and took our sins and rose again. This is what Christianity is about. And whether you're Catholic or Protestant, we agree in the centrality of the cross, that there something supernatural happened that could affect you and me in 1969.

## February 2, 1969

Prelude

Opening Remarks                    THE PRESIDENT

Doxology

Prayer    THE REVEREND DR. RICHARD C. HALVERSON
Fourth Presbyterian Church
Washington, D.C.

Hymn                              *"Faith of Our Fathers"*

Solo                               Mr. JAMES MCDONALD
*"The Prodigal"*

Sermon

Hymn                    *"The Church's One Foundation"*

Benediction

Postlude

# The Reverend Dr. Richard C. Halverson

THE PRESIDENT: Mrs. Nixon and I are very happy to welcome all of you to this worship service in the White House. And we are privileged today to have with us, to conduct our service, Dr. Richard Halverson of the Fourth Presbyterian Church of Washington, D.C. Dr. Halverson, incidentally, includes in his large congregation Secretary of Defense Melvin Laird and Senator Mark Hatfield, both of whom are in attendance this morning. And for the music part of our service today we are happy to have James McDonald. Mr. McDonald is known to many of you, I am sure, as one of the great spiritual singers of this world. He has just recently returned from Vietnam, and he is now engaged in a very effective program, traveling all over the country in the interest of better relations between races—accomplishing his mission through the medium of religion through song.

DR. HALVERSON: We thank thee, our Father in heaven, for the privilege of meeting in this place in the name of Jesus Christ, mindful of his promise to be in our midst whenever we gather in his name. We thank thee for thy presence, for thy love, and for the expectation we feel as we wait upon thee that we may be equipped to serve thee and our fellow man in the week to come. May thy Spirit now move upon us and satisfy all that we need, to the glory of Jesus Christ, in whose name we pray. Amen.

11

Mr. President and Mrs. Nixon, ladies and gentlemen, greetings in the name of our Lord, Jesus Christ. Yesterday I received in the mail a letter from a friend in Madras, India, dated January 26. I want to read just a few sentences from this letter: "Last Sunday I had four important services in addition to the evening crusade meeting. Knowing Richard Nixon was to be inaugurated the next day, I requested bishops, pastors, and people to pray for him. They were all so thrilled to be asked and they not only prayed then but said they would continue to pray for him and our nation." He continued, "I have felt today a great longing in my heart to encourage our President by prayer." It seemed to me providential that this letter should have come yesterday.

At the time of our election last November, I was in Singapore for the first All-Asia South Pacific Congress on Evangelism. (I voted by absentee ballot, by the way.) And the thing that interested the few of us from the West who were there (there were thirty-six Western observers) was the interest and concern in the election taking place in the United States. There was a large blackboard in the center of the huge hall around which the auditoriums and smaller meeting rooms were located, and as news of the election progressed, it was registered on this blackboard. Always there was a great crowd of Asians around the board—so much so that often we from the United States were unable to get near enough to find out what was happening. When the news of the election was final, the Congress had prayer which was joined in by the twelve hundred delegates from Asia and the South Pacific as well as the thirty-six Western observers.

Though this has nothing to do with my remarks this morning, fervently we thank God for this concern on the part of the whole world—a concern that manifested itself in prayer for leadership in the United States. I think it is important for men and women in places of leadership to know that they are being sustained by prayer, that there are those Christian people of all denominational labels who feel it is their responsibility to sustain you in prayer as you take office—and they are faithful in it.

May I ask you to bow your heads for just a moment of prayer, please. Let the words of my mouth and the meditation of our hearts be acceptable in thy sight, O Lord, our Strength and our Redeemer. Amen.

I'd like to take a text this morning and then depart from it—which some have said is therefore a pretext—but come back to it at the conclusion. The Apostle Paul had a remarkable gift for stating profound truth in great brevity. And this is one of the examples of this ability: in II Corinthians 1:20, he records, "For all the promises of God in [Christ] are yea, and in him Amen, unto the glory of God by us." One of the vernacular translations, the J. B. Phillips version, puts that text this way: "Christ . . . is the divine 'Yes.' Every promise of God finds its affirmative in him." Another puts it: "All God's provisions have their yes in Jesus Christ."

It has been my experience in the pastorate that thoughtful people think of faith, Christian faith, or religious faith in general, primarily in terms of responsibility to God, to fellow man, to their own family and home, and to themselves personally. They strive to be the best kind of person possible, maximizing their own personal potential, fulfilling their role in life.

But two attitudes in extreme are often taken on this matter of responsibility. One is that of abdication. There are many—a fact tragically confirmed in history and contemporary times—who make bold their profession but allow a gross disparity between their profession and their practice. They think of religion in general or Christian faith in particular as having to do with re-sponsibility, then abdicate this responsibility. Their lives are characterized by indifference, by coasting in a kind of downhill existence.

At the other extreme are those who take their responsibility very seriously and become so immersed in their duty that they begin to think that all of the resources to fulfill this responsibility are somehow their own. They forget the equipment which God has provided, the gifts with which God endowed them at birth, the life which God gives them and the environment in which God has placed them. They forget God and assume that all of their exploits are accomplished by their own efforts and energies and resources. They give themselves the credit for taking their responsibilities so seriously. And this can happen not only to a person but to a society as well. We so easily forget the God who gave us all we have with which to work, all the raw materials by which to fulfill the responsibility into which He has placed us.

This is equally dangerous, because suddenly the man is trusting in himself and ignoring God. The only faith he has is in himself, no longer in God. A nation may do this to its doom, forget the God who made it great and assume that somehow its greatness is endemic in its own virtue rather than in the sustaining love and providence of God.

Therefore I should like to suggest that there is another way to look at Christian faith which is as fundamental as responsibility. Christianity has to do with resources, divine resources. Surprisingly, in twenty-six years of ministry I have found this a rather rare way of looking at the Christian faith, recognizing that God has provided resources for man by which he is able to fulfill his responsibility. And I would like to suggest some of those resources which God makes available.

First, there is His promise (and these resources are all expressed in the Bible in terms of promises—God's provision comes through God's promises). There is the promise to sustain us in the hour of trial and trouble and tragedy. "Cast thy burden upon the Lord, and he shall sustain thee." When we cast our burden on the Lord, this does not therefore free us to abdicate responsibility. Indeed, the very opposite occurs. The man who has learned to cast his burden upon the Lord finds himself being electrified by the power of God so that he is increasingly efficient to fulfill his responsibility in that situation. But he learns to draw upon the strength and power from God.

There are many kinds of burdens which we may cast upon the Lord. There is the burden of guilt, which one psychologist has called the most corrosive influence in life. It is impossible to measure the destruction that results from guilt: the husbands and wives that are estranged, parents and children that are alienated, businesses that are destroyed, man hours that are lost by the gradual eating away of one's efficiency because of inward gnawing which erodes all of the vitality of his life.

This is a burden which God uniquely specializes in bearing for men. The elderly Apostle John made this marvelous promise: "If we confess our sins, he is faithful and just to forgive us our sins, and to cleanse us from all unrighteousness." This was, of course, expressed in the beautiful song which Jimmy McDonald sang this morning. And it is a picture of us as human beings. It is a parable of this very message. And by the way, Jimmy and I did not compare notes ahead of time. Here was a son who said to his father, "Give me what is mine." The father did so and the son went into a far country and wasted it, ending up in a pig pen—and "would fain have filled his belly with the husks that the swine did eat."

Finally he came to himself—the Scripture makes a point of this —and began to be honest with himself about himself and he said, "The servants in my father's household are better off than I. I'm going back and ask to be a servant." He went back to apologize, to confess to his father and say, "Let me be a servant in your home." The father, "seeing his son a great way off"—he must have stood by that door watching the path to the horizon until the son would return—rushed out to meet him, threw his arms around him, and with great affection brought him home. There he put on him the best robes, killed the fatted calf, put the finest jewelry on his fingers, and celebrated. The son who was lost, had been found—who was dead, was now alive.

This is a picture of God's concern for the sinner. All God asks is that he come to himself, that he be honest with himself about himself and say, "I'm not worthy." And when he comes to God on this basis, God throws His arms around him, covers him with His love, and puts on him the garment of salvation. The Word of God teaches that it is pride—a strange, stubborn, ridiculous pride—that keeps a man, especially one who is so capable of fulfilling his responsibility, from admittting his need of God's forgiveness. Certainly the responsible Christian will take relief from the burden of guilt in the love of God by coming to Him and asking forgiveness.

In this context I have been thinking about the power of His presence. If the President will excuse me, I think of this a great deal—of the loneliness of the man in leadership. After all the counsel and all the intelligence has been given, and he has listened, finally there is no place else to go for the decision. He is alone and he must make it, right or wrong, whatever the results, he must make it. (I believe it was President Truman who had a sign on his desk, "The buck stops here.") But actually he is not alone. There is One there, though invisible, who loves him and understands, who is the Lord of history. He is available. That is the incredible fact for men in high places of responsibility, the availability of God to be there anytime He is needed. That is the ultimate Resource.

Then there is the resource of wisdom. The wisest men are the humblest, because they have succeeded in learning that there is so much more that is unknown in relation to what they know. As the diameter of one's knowledge increases, the circumference of his ignorance increases geometrically. The wise man is humble. As the great scientist said near his death, "I stand on the edge of the ocean of knowledge. I have a teacup of knowledge in my mind. There lies the vast ocean still to be discovered." There come times when we need the wisdom of God, and James, the very practical disciple of Jesus, has promised us, "If any of you lack wisdom, let him ask of God, that giveth to all men liberally, and upbraideth not; and it shall be given him."

However, here again human pride is self-defeating. Sometimes the hardest thing we have to do is to admit we lack wisdom and then ask for it. But this is one of the resources of God for men in very troubled times. All one needs to do is to admit his lack, ask, and God will provide His wisdom.

There is a third resource which is direction. Who of us has not wondered which way do I go next? Even the wisest of us sometimes is troubled by confusion and perplexity. But the Bible abounds in promises in which God says that He will direct our steps: "Commit thy way unto the Lord; trust also in him; and he shall bring it to pass." Or another from Proverbs which is guaranteed to lead out of bewilderment: "Trust in the Lord with all thine heart; and lean not unto thine own understanding. In all thy ways acknowledge him, and he shall direct thy paths." The Psalmist declares, "The steps of a good man are ordered by the Lord: and he delighteth in his way." Another, "Commit thy works unto the Lord, and thy thoughts shall be established." You may not know how God is leading, but you can know He is! In every step you take, every thought you think, God will give you direction. This is His resource.

Finally, there is His strength—strength for the day. "As thy days, so shall thy strength be." Men in leadership are drained of strength, not only daily, but hourly at times, under the pressure of circumstances and responsibility—until they are literally physically unable to go on. But there is a remarkable promise in the Word of God, that He will give strength to the weak. And you can receive this strength and be infused literally with the strength of God in the time of powerlessness.

The Apostle Paul, one of the most brilliant minds the human race has ever produced, experienced this. He shares with us in his second letter to the Corinthians the fact that he was given "a thorn in the flesh." He does not tell us what it was. He calls it "the messenger of Satan to buffet me." But he says three times he asked God to remove this thorn in the flesh. He said it was given, incidentally, "lest I be exalted above measure," for he was the great Apostle, writing more than half of the New Testament. And this was a messenger to humble him, to keep him from being overly exalted because of his significant role in apostolic church history.

Three times he asked God to remove this thorn in the flesh, but the answer that God gave him was not to remove the thorn, rather He urged him to discover the adequacy of the Grace of God. God said to Paul, "My grace is sufficient for thee: for my strength is made perfect in weakness." Paul testified—and I know there are some in our sophisticated contemporary age who think that he must have been a pathological case—nevertheless he testified, "I therefore rejoice in infirmities and I take pleasure in weakness because when I am weak, then am I strong." You know, it is impossible to be too weak for God, but it is easy to be too strong for God. This great Apostle, the major interpreter of the faith that was in Jesus Christ, who planted the church throughout Asia Minor and in Europe, who was probably as responsible as any other man for Western civilization, this great Apostle Paul said, "When I am weak, then am I strong."

Well . . . even the greatest of men and the strongest of men have their weaknesses, and it is important to remember at the point of weakness that the strength of God is available if we are willing to admit our need and receive His strength.

Now I return to the text with which I began—"All God's promises have their yes in Jesus Christ." I have given you only a few of the promises from the Scriptures. I could continue for hours with great and relevant promises which offer the resources of God to responsible men in order that they may fulfill their responsibility to the maximum. But I have been only suggestive. Yet all of these promises, all of these provisions, all of the resources which God proffers, He has wrapped up in His Son, Jesus Christ. And when you have the Son, you have everything God gives. In the final analysis, this matter of faith is a matter of cultivating a personal relationship with the Son of God, Jesus Christ. When you have Christ and Christ has you, when you are His and He is yours, then all of the resources of God are available on request to be appropriated.

I suppose the saddest words in the Bible were those penned by the Apostle John in the prologue to his Gospel, when he wrote, "He [Jesus Christ] was in the world, and the world was made by him, and the world knew him not. He came unto his own, and his own received him not. But as many as received him, to them gave he power to become the sons of God." This is fundamental to responsible Christian leadership, to acknowledge one's need of God and to find that need adequately supplied in the Son of God. To receive Christ, to believe on his name, is the way of wisdom, strength, and adequacy.

Forgive us, O God, our pride that would reject God's provision. Help us who are strong, who are wise, who are well endowed, never to forget the God who made it so. And may we realize that when we kneel to God, we stand tall. Give us the grace in our sense of responsibility to receive humbly the resources of God in Christ to fulfill it. Let thy blessing abide upon this nation and the world. We pray in Jesus' name. Amen.

# March 16, 1969

Prelude

Opening Remarks                        THE PRESIDENT

Doxology

Prayer          THE REVEREND DR. LOUIS H. EVANS, JR.
                          La Jolla Presbyterian Church
                          La Jolla, California

Hymn                    *"Praise Ye the Lord, the Almighty"*

Choir           Members of the Junior Boys' Choir of
                          The Washington Cathedral
                          *"Jesu, Joy of Man's Desiring"*
                          by Johann Sebastian Bach

Sermon                  *"Identity Crisis: Who Are You?"*

Hymn                    *"Crown Him with Many Crowns"*

Benediction

Postlude

The one dozen boys from the Junior Boys' Choir of
The Washington Cathedral range in age from 7 to 12
years. They sing 3 services each week. The choir has
been singing since the Cathedral opened in 1907.

# The Reverend Dr. Louis H. Evans, Jr.

THE PRESIDENT: Thirty-six years ago when I was attending college, a very exciting and inspiring speaker addressed us at one of our services—a young minister, Dr. Louis Evans. I never forgot the man or what he said, and he had great influence on my life.

Immediately after the election this past year, we flew to San Diego, California, and the first religious service that we attended was at the La Jolla Presbyterian Church. The speaker was a young, exciting, and inspiring man, Dr. Louis Evans, *Jr.*

Dr. Louis Evans, Jr. will conduct the worship services this morning.

DR. EVANS: Our God and Father, we need not beg you to be present here, for you have promised that where two or three are gathered in your name, you are in their midst. So we gratefully acknowledge your presence with us. You have wanted us to have fullness of life, and so you have told us to love you with all our heart, soul, strength, and mind, and then to love others in the same way in which we love ourselves.

Forgive us, therefore, O Father, when we have rejected you by not thanking you for the creation you have made or for the leadership you offer. Forgive us when we have degraded or belittled ourselves or hurt others around us. We desire to make these things right. So help us to walk in the assurance that once we have honestly admitted these things and given them to you, we *are* forgiven. We also pray for each other in these days of heavy responsibilities of leadership. May we do these jobs —no matter how important or lowly the task may be—without a sense of superiority or inferiority, realizing that each has his place, that the

21

team would not be complete without any one of us. May we do our tasks with the joy of knowing that we are needed, that others are about us to fill in where we cannot and thus we complement one another.

Above all, O Father, give us love. A love that can be expressed for you, for ourselves, and for one another through Jesus Christ our Lord. Amen.

Perhaps one of the most personal and intimate passages in all of Scripture is an encounter that Jesus Christ had with his disciples the night before he was to be betrayed; the next day he was crucified! He had told his disciples that he was going to Jerusalem to suffer at the hands of the religious and political leaders, and of course this message filled them with a tremendous sense of foreboding and trouble. They had attached themselves to this man, they had hoped that he would be their political as well as religious leader, and now he had said he was going to die. It is no wonder, then, that great sorrow filled their hearts, and after speaking to them those very familiar words about his Father's house having many mansions or rooms, he then told them that he was going to prepare a place for them. He added that they knew where he was going and the way there, but Thomas, who was prone to doubting, said to him, "Lord, we do not know where you are going; how can we know the way?"

And Jesus said to him, "I am the way, the truth, and the life. No man comes to the Father except by me, and if you had known me you would have known my Father also, and henceforth you will see him and know him."

And then Philip said to him, "But Lord, show us the Father and then we will be satisfied."

And Jesus said, "Have I been so long with you and yet you have not known me, Philip? He who has seen me has seen the Father. How then can you say, 'show us the Father'? Do you not believe that I am in the Father and the Father is in me? The words I speak I do not speak on my own authority, but I do the works of Him who sent me. Now, believe me that I am in the Father and the

Father is in me, or else believe me for the sake of these very works themselves."

This morning, because I was told this is to be an informal occasion, I am going to do something that isn't often done in sermons. I am going to take somebody from the audience and speak to him, and because I know one of the men in the third row here, I am going to speak to you, Herb Klein. Is that all right? I've nurtured his soul carefully these last years. Herb, suppose I were to tell you that I was going to paint a portrait of you and that wherever you went I wanted you to put this portrait in front of you because I like you. I want people to know you as *I* know you, and wherever you go when people see this portrait they will know you. They will know how you feel, they will know how you think, they will know what you are like just by my portrait of you, and you will need nothing other than that portrait. Will you go for that? [Mr. Klein hesitated, and then answered "all right."]

You will? Well, I wouldn't. I don't think I would want anybody to know me by someone else's portrait of me. I want to be known for myself, because there are things that no one can see about me, things that only I can tell others about myself. And I think we all should insist upon this privilege of establishing our own relationships with other people. Are we in agreement, Herb? [Smiling, Mr. Klein readily agreed.]

All right. And if others insist on portraying us as something we are not, if they insist on determining how others are to view us, then is it any wonder we feel misunderstood, lonely, rejected, and even angry? And rightly so—for this would be a crisis in identity!

Have you ever stopped to think that Jesus Christ had an identity crisis? Few could see him for who he really was because of their portraits of preconception.

Now, there were in Jesus' day those who were looking for the Messiah—the Messiah who the Jews believed would lead them out from under bondage. They had been in political bondage for seven centuries. They had been passed along by five major empires. They knew a brief century of liberty, but then they lost it as the Romans took them over in a hardfisted tyranny. Is it any wonder, then, that the Jews were looking for the Messiah in the form of a militaristic leader? They got their nationalism all mixed up in their religion. Therefore, when Jesus the Messiah came and said that he was going to suffer and die, we can understand that the disciples wouldn't accept this kind of a Messiah. No, he couldn't be a suffering Messiah. This didn't fit their portrait of preconception.

And there was another group among the Jews. They were the Pharisees. They were the legalists obsessed on obeying the thousand little religious laws, and they would wave their fingers of judgment at anybody who broke these laws. When Jesus did not pass judgment on the wayward as defined by these laws, they opposed him. They rejected him. Yes, they even crucified him because "he was tearing down the structure of Moses," they said. They could not see him because of their preconception.

Even today we paint portraits of Jesus. The galleries of mankind are full of them. Let's look at some of these portraits. Picture ourselves walking through a gallery. Now here's one. Sweet Jesus, meek and mild. The picture is done in soft pastels, Jesus is holding a lamb in his arms. He's very bland in his smile. You're not even sure whether he is male or female. Children who learn only this picture of Jesus can never really understand the Jesus of anger or the Jesus of strength.

Let us move on to the next picture. Here is one quite the opposite. Jesus the social reformer. In the background are factories belching smoke into smog-clogged skies. Jesus' sleeves are rolled up like the other workers who stride abreast of him, marching on the bastions of capitalism. For this Jesus there is no time for anything but social reformation.

Then we come to the third portrait. Another contrast. Jesus the gentleman. The scene is a social hour in some plush drawing-room. You can tell that a ripple of delicate social laughter is

running among the guests. The face of the hostess exudes an air
that no controversy will be permitted in this delightful meeting
of the saints.

And here's another portrait: "Jesus and the Disciples in the
Devotional Hour." The artist shows Jesus sitting on a pastoral
hilltop surrounded by a carpet of wild flowers amidst his adoring
disciples who are gazing transfixed into his mystical face, so
thoroughly absorbed in this relationship that they cannot hear
the cries of the city below, grim with hunger, with the grime of
poverty and war.

How many portraits are there? We could spend hours going
through this gallery. We notice that clusters of people are worshiping in front of each of these portraits, and if Jesus himself
were to walk through the halls of that gallery they probably would
not recognize him, so bent are they on the portraits. Couldn't
they see him? No, in all probability they couldn't see him because
he would be hidden by a forest of portraits—the portraits of
nationalists, of legalists, of pietists, of revolutionaries, of the
power hungry.

I wonder how Jesus would feel. Doesn't he give us a clue here
in this chapter? Obviously, by their questions the disciples had
not yet fully recognized who Jesus was. Here he was God's own
self-portrait, God's self-disclosure, but Philip could not recognize him, Peter could not recognize him. And so Philip asked
Jesus to put God on display; the Greek word used here in the
Gospel of John is "to make an exhibit of him," as though you
could put a puppet on a stage or draw a diagram or make some
mechanical representation of God! And Philip said, "Jesus, do
this and then we'll be satisfied." Satisfied with a mechanical display? Never!

Jesus' response was one of anguish and hurt and one of the
most poignant questions ever asked in the New Testament:
"Have I been so long with you and yet you have not recognized
who I am, Philip? Do you not see me as God's own self-disclo-

sure? If you have really recognized who I am, then you have seen the Father. How then can you say, 'Show us the Father'?"

You see, they had missed the point that in Jesus Christ God is saying, "Here I am in terms you can understand, terms of flesh and blood"—because, you see, Jesus Christ is God's semantic breakthrough. He is God's personal vehicle of dialogue. The question is today, as we are confronted with this person of Jesus Christ, what are we accepting; what are we rejecting—a portrait?

And you young people, this is a day when you want to know other people for whom they really are. Can we really let Jesus be who he is? Isn't that the question of all society? Can we accept ourselves for what we truly are? Can we accept others for what they truly are?

For instance, can world leaders hear other leaders, hear what they are saying and notice what they are feeling, or do years or even centuries of bitterness and misunderstanding distort and create a false portrait?

Can a husband accept a wife for her strength and her weakness, or can a wife accept her husband for what he is? Or must they respond to some image they have painted of each other out of their own need—and thus are disappointed when their partner does not live up to their expectation?

Can a white society really accept a black, brown, or red-skinned person for what he really is—a human being with a personal potential given him by the Creator, a person who has a hunger to become the productive and proud human being that God meant him to become? Or will the society respond to some stereotype portrait drawn in the ink of supposed superiority or guilt?

Can parents discover the real child? Each child is a rare combination of potentials and weaknesses. Can they help that child to understand his potential and to develop it, to give it to humanity for creativity? Or will they press upon that child some familiar image drawn by Aunt Susie or Uncle Hal and in doing so irreparably damage that little life?

And is this not the cry of the world? Is it not the same anguished question that Jesus asked of his disciples? "Have I been so long with you and yet you have not known me?"

Recently in my own marriage I have been learning in fresh ways to discover a beautiful woman with whom God has given me the joy of walking through life. In the past, I used to be angry when she wasn't quite what I wanted in mechanical abilities, but now I am discovering that maybe *her* weaknesses are an area where my strength can have meaning. And whenever we get into a crowd, one of *my* weaknesses is failing to remember people's names; so I nudge her for her strength, and she gives the proper name at the proper time. And so strengths and weaknesses begin to dovetail together to create a teamwork; I am not trying to ask of her things she was not meant to give. It is a new relationship. It was always great, but it's getting better.

And what about Christ? Well, I used to respond to Christ more out of an acceptance of theological propositions about him, propositions that other people had created. But now I see that he is one to be known as a person who can enter into personal relationship with us. Is not this what the Bible says all the way through? God is a God who approaches His people where they are to be known for who He is. He says, "I want to be your God, and I want you to be my people."

What sweeping, healing reforms would come to this world if sections of our society were to cast off the false portraits they have of others and discover persons for what they truly are—and then accept them and help them to develop their own specialities for the benefit of a great nation. That *would* be a revolution, a revolution of joy, wouldn't it?

And to Christ how would we answer the question, "Have I been so long with you and yet you have not known me?" You know Jesus has been around for a long time, but I wonder how many of us see him for who he really is. Can we enter into a relationship with him so that we will permit him to do what only he can accomplish ultimately—to free us from our sin and guilt; to give us love to replace hate, honesty that flushes away preconception, a personal encounter that surpasses any portrait or introduction by another? Can we really know him as a Christ who can be intensely personal and yet amazingly global, a Christ who is friend, who is leader, who is worthy of being crowned king? "Have I been so long with you and yet you have not known me?" Why not ask him to speak for himself?

# *April 27, 1969*

Prelude

Opening Remarks                          THE PRESIDENT

Doxology

Prayer            THE REVEREND DR. EDWARD G. LATCH
                  Chaplain, U.S. House of Representatives

Hymn                *"Holy, Holy, Holy! Lord God Almighty"*

Solo                              MR. ROBERT NICHOLSON
                  *"The Lord is My Light"* by Francis Allitsen

Sermon

Hymn                     *"God of Grace and God of Glory"*

Benediction

Postlude

---

Mr. Nicholson was born in Sydney, Australia, and came to the United States in 1936 to study music. He was a member of the Metropolitan Opera Association for the Spring season of 1939 and in later years sang with Eileen Farrell on CBS. He is presently soloist for the Wesley United Methodist Church in Washington, D.C.

# The Reverend Dr. Edward G. Latch

THE PRESIDENT: This year the Metropolitan Memorial Church in Wesley Heights is celebrating its 100th Anniversary. For twenty-six of those hundred years Dr. Edward Latch was the minister, and for four of those hundred years the Nixon family, when we lived in Wesley Heights, attended that church and there came to know him, his wife, and his family very well and to respect and love them.

In 1960 when I was nominated for the Presidency for the first time, he gave the benediction at the conclusion of the acceptance speech. You can see how our lives have been together, and now when I return to Washington I find him in the place where I first came in. He is the Chaplain of the Congress of the United States, the House of Representatives, and we are delighted that he is able to join us this morning and to conduct our worship service.

DR. LATCH: The President referred to the fact that I offered the closing prayer at the Republican National Convention in 1960. I offered the prayer, I remember, and gave the benediction which I was requested to do: "The Lord bless thee and keep thee," and then I went on to say, "Give thee peace"—and how these words slipped out, I do not know—"and give thee peace *and victory.*" I think the Lord tapped me on the shoulder and said something like this: "That was a good prayer, my son, but we'll wait eight years."

Almighty God, our heavenly Father, who art the source of all our being, the goal of every noble endeavor, and the companion of our way, in the quiet of this moment we pause in thy presence, acknowledging our dependence upon thee and offering unto thee once again the devotion and the gratitude of our hearts. We thank thee for our nation, and pray that thou will grant unto our President, his Cabinet, the members of Congress, the Supreme Court, and all who lead us, wisdom, understanding, and insight that they may lead our nation in the ways of peace. We pray for our people that we may learn to live together in an abiding spirit of good will.

We thank thee for those in the armed forces of our country throughout our world, living for, dying for, fighting for this land we love with all our hearts. Strengthen them in danger, comfort them in sorrow, keep them ever true in the performance of duty and ever loyal to this land we love. We thank thee for our homes and for the affection of the domestic fireside, for the freedom to worship and for all the freedoms that are ours.

Accept our gratitude for thy goodness. Make us daily aware of thy presence and enable us to go forth from this service into the days of this week to face our responsibilities and our tasks, knowing and believing that thou art with us and that with thee all good things are possible. In the spirit of Jesus Christ our Lord, we pray. Amen.


Some time ago a minister gave an address to the students of the American College in Beirut, Lebanon. In that body of students there were representatives of some sixteen different religious faiths. In fact, the minister claimed you could fairly feel these faiths bristling at one another. Being a wise man, he began his address by saying, "I am not going to ask any one of you to change your religious faith, but I am asking each one of you to face this question honestly: *What is your religious faith doing to you?*" They were ready to argue for their faith, ready to defend it, but what an entirely different story they had to tell when on the plane of experience they were asked to say what their religious faith was actually doing to them.

This is the question I want to raise in your thinking as we worship together in the White House this morning. What is your religious faith doing to you? There are, of course, many things our faith can do for us. For one thing, it can sound deep down in our lives the note of joy. I feel and I believe that we ought to be a happy people, a genuinely happy people, because we are followers of the Great Nazarene. There is an old Gospel hymn some of us used to sing: "You may have the joy bells ringing in your heart, / And a peace that from you never will depart; / Walk the straight and narrow way, / Live for Jesus every day; / He will keep the joy bells ringing in your heart."

That is what our religious faith can do for us—sound deep down in life the note of joy. And yet when you look at some religious people, how gloomy many of them are, how dismal their appearance, how pessimistic their mood, how negative their spirit! Lady Astor is reported to have called Dean Inge of London a gloomy man, believing in a gloomy God. This is not altogether fair to the Dean, but it does aptly describe the attitude and spirit of many people today. Go beneath the surface of our modern culture and you will find people of plenty who have just enough religion to make them unhappy; just enough belief in God, just enough perception of the moral law, just enough vision of a better life, just enough faith in the life which is to come, that they cannot live like some of the pagans around them and be happy about it. They have not achieved what I might call the reality of a radiant faith.

They are something like Charles Sturgeon, a famous Baptist minister, who was talking to a group of divinity students and was trying to get across the idea that you should let your life reflect what you are saying. When you talk about heaven, he said, let your face light up with a heavenly glory; when you talk about hell, your everyday face will do. And the everyday face of all too many of us is precisely like that. We have enough religion to make us miserable but not enough to make us magnificent; enough to

make life depressing but not enough to make it a delight; enough
to make it pessimistic but not enough to make it optimistic.

When we have enough of this reality we call religion, it sounds
deep in life a note of joy. It was so with Jesus. In a way, he was
the most joyful person the world has ever seen. He began his
ministry with these words: "Blessed are the poor in spirit. . . .
Blessed are they that mourn." The word "blessed" is this deep
note of joy. At the very end, he said, "These things have I spoken
unto you, that my joy might remain in you, and that your joy
might be made full." Underlying his life like a deep current there
was this note of joy.

At the end of the parable of the Prodigal Son, are the words,
"and they began to be merry." That is the keynote of the Kingdom of Heaven. "Joy," said Dean Inge, "is the sign of the tri-
umph of life, the sign that we are living our lives as spiritual
beings." Now, this is what our faith can do for us—sound deep
in life the note of joy.

Then, too, it can sound the note of courage. Courage, for one
thing, to face life with all of its troubles and with all of its temptations. My soul, we do have troubles and we do have temptations
in this day. We need an inner Spirit to help us meet them—not
only meet them but manage them, and not only manage them but
master them. There are those who think of religion as an escape
from life, an evading of reality, a running away from the hard
facts of our existence. But when our religious faith is real, it is
anything but that.

Said the Apostle: "In him who strengthens me, I am able for
anything." Come on, Life, say your best word or your worst, your
first word or your last—I can take what I am called upon to take.
I can endure what I must endure. I can overcome what it is
possible for me to overcome, not in my own unaided strength but
through the strength of Him who lives in my heart. Says the
Apostle in Phillips' translation, "I am ready for anything through
the strength of the one who lives within me." Through that

strength we are given courage, courage to face life clearly, strongly, and with peace, knowing we do not face it alone.

Our faith also gives us courage to do what we believe to be right. I do not know what to think of this so-called new morality. I have the feeling that it is not new at all. I think it is nothing more than the old immorality. We put a miniskirt on it and say it's living in the twentieth century. No, it is nothing but the old immorality over and over again.

There *is* a moral law. Goodness and truth and beauty live at the very basis of the structure of the universe in which we live. There are some things in life of which we should be aware and adjust ourselves to rather than to be forever rearranging them for our own use. You do not rearrange a moral law. You adjust yourself to it and you live. If you do not adjust yourself, if you try to rearrange it, ultimately you die.

I know we have the feeling sometimes that . . . well, we can always vote and that will take care of everything. Now, voting has its place in its right sphere, but that doesn't make anything right. A teacher brought two little bunnies into the classroom to show the class, and the children were talking about them. Then someone asked the teacher whether they were boy bunnies or girl bunnies. The teacher didn't know, and the children didn't know. Finally some child said, "Let's vote on it." We can vote, but there are certain things in life that are unchanging no matter how we may vote.

What I am trying to say is simply this: Let us learn to stand for what we believe is right. Our beloved General Eisenhower, when he was President, one time said, "This I did for no other reason than I believed it to be the right thing to do." That is precisely what I am talking about—the courage to do what we firmly and honestly believe to be right. This is what our faith builds into our lives.

There is one other thing our religion does for us—it sounds deep in our lives the note of good will. If there is any one thing we need in our day and in our generation, it is this spirit of good will. We may walk along different paths, believe different things, but underlying all our differences we ought to keep sounding, and keep alive within us, the refrain of good will. I believe the survival of our nation depends ultimately upon the good will we maintain and cultivate in this day in which we are living. Good will among churches, good will among races, good will among groups and classes, good will everywhere. This is primarily the duty of the home, the church, and the school, and I hope they will not abdicate but will assume the responsibility of teaching us how to live together in this great land that we love with all our hearts. We must wake up to this spirit of good will. May I tell you the story of an elderly couple way up in their eighties who lived in a home for the aging? They thought they would go on a date—have a dinner and go to a movie. So they did. The gentleman was dressed and ready in no time, but of course, the ladies in the home all came to help the lady get dressed. They put a little corsage on her dress, a little ribbon in her hair, and then said to her that when she came home, she must tell them everything that happened. The couple left around 5:30, had dinner, went to the early show, and came back around 10:00 P.M.

That was enough for the gentleman—up to bed he went. But the ladies gathered around the other lady and asked what did he do, what did he say, what did you do, what did you say? And she said, "You know something, I had to slap him three times." All agog, they asked what happened, what happened? She said, "I thought he was dead."

What I am trying to say is that someone needs to stimulate in us the spirit of good will. We must never be dead to good will, because if we are, then we are dead, although we may walk around a little while longer. We must keep the spirit of good will alive in our lives together as a nation, and then show to the world that amid differences we can and we will get along together.

Joy and courage and good will are the fruits of religious faith and they begin with ourselves. I heard a story of a young man on a college campus who began shouting that now we are going to make the nation clean, we're going to tidy up this city of ours. His father came up to him afterward and said, "Son, I'm so glad to hear you say that. Now let's begin with your own room."

Precisely! It begins with ourselves, this whole sense of joy and courage and good will. It will come as we learn to commit ourselves to the highest and the best that we know—when we commit ourselves to God and let Him have His way with our own lives. Not by forming resolutions to be more joyful, more courageous, more filled with good will, not by saying we will try harder to be more joyful, more courageous, more filled with good will will they come, but by a commitment, a personal commitment of our lives to Jesus Christ. Then by giving him his chance through daily prayer, daily reading of his Word, daily living at our best, and daily sharing our lives with those about us—out of this commitment will come joy in living, courage for life, and an enthusiasm for good will. May our faith begin more than ever to do that for us and in us and through us.

Grant, our Father, that we may so commit our lives anew unto thee that thy spirit may develop within us the deep note of joy and courage and good will which we may share with others and as a nation share with our world. Amen.

# May 4, 1969

Prelude

Opening Remarks                    THE PRESIDENT

Doxology

Prayer                             DR. R. H. EDWIN ESPY
                                   General Secretary
                           National Council of Churches

Hymn                               *"Faith of Our Fathers"*

Choir              COLUMBIA UNION COLLEGE PRO MUSICA
                   *"Awake, My Heart"* by Jane Marshall
                                   Director: Paul Hill
                           Accompanist: Star Stevens

Sermon                      "Faith and Works are One"

Hymn                          *"How Firm a Foundation"*

Choral Benediction              *"The Lord Bless You and
                                              Keep You"*
                                   by Peter Lutkin

Postlude

The Pro Musica is the most active of the four choral
groups included within the music department of Columbia Union College in Takoma Park, Maryland.
This group has toured extensively on the East Coast
and has sung on nationwide television. Their director,
Paul Hill, is also Musical Director of the National
Choral Foundation, Inc.

# Dr. R. H. Edwin Espy

THE PRESIDENT: We are very happy to welcome you to the White House for our Sunday Worship Service on this beautiful spring morning. Conducting our service today is Dr. Edwin Espy, who is the General Secretary of the National Council of Churches. I find, incidentally, that we have something in common. We both went to college in California; he attended Redlands University and was the champion debater there just shortly before and perhaps somewhat overlapping the time that I attended Whittier College. Redlands, as I told him, had the reputation of producing the finest speakers in all of the Southern California Conference. I know we will enjoy hearing him this morning, and we are grateful for his participation in our service.

DR. ESPY: Lord, our heavenly Father, Almighty and Everlasting God, who has safely brought us to the beginning of this day, defend us in the same with thy mighty power and grant that on this day we fall into no sin. And may all our doings be righteous in thy sight, through Jesus Christ our Lord. Amen.

O Lord, our heavenly Father, the High and Mighty Ruler of the Universe, who doth from thy throne behold all the dwellers upon earth, most heartily we beseech thee with thy favor to behold and bless thy servant, Richard Nixon, the President of the United States, and all others in authority, and so replenish them with the grace of thy Holy Spirit that they may always incline to thy will and walk in thy way. Imbue them plenteously with heavenly gifts. Grant them, in health and prosperity,

39

long to live and finally after this life to attain everlasting joy and felicity
through Jesus Christ our Lord. Amen.

I am sure I speak on behalf of all of us who are here in expressing our sense of indebtedness and gratitude for the beautiful
choral music we have heard in this service. Since this is a group
of young people associated with an institution of higher education, I should like to center my meditation this morning on a
personal experience from my life as a graduate student many
years ago in Germany.

The theme is faith and works. There is a passage in the Bible
that is familiar to all of us, from the Epistle of James, the second
chapter, which I should like to read to you at the outset. James
writes, "What does it profit, my brethen, if a man says he has faith
but has not works? Can his faith save him? If a brother or sister
is ill-clad and in lack of daily food, and one of you says to them,
'Go in peace, be warmed and filled,' without giving them the
things needed for the body, what does it profit?"

So faith by itself, if it has no works, is dead, just as the body
apart from the spirit is dead. Faith is completed by works.

It was my privilege many years ago, after completing my studies at Union Theological Seminary in New York, to spend some
two and a half years in graduate work in Germany. It was the
period of the middle thirties when Hitler was consolidating his
power. I had arrived in Germany in July of 1933, was at the
University of Tübingen for some three semesters, and then at the
University of Heidelberg.

This was about thirty-four years ago, before the members of
this choir this morning were born. While in Heidelberg, I was
rooming with a young German who was an energetic student. He
was a man who according to his own lights had character. He was
attractive, he was popular, he was a fanatical National Socialist.
He had a particular professor for whom he had high regard and
respect. From time to time, he would take occasion to extol the

virtues of this professor. I remember how on one occasion he said that if it had not been for this member of the faculty, he would have chucked his college course overboard long ago and would have left the life of the university. But this one superior teacher kept him going.

One day, however, this student came to me in great perturbation and said, "Ed, I don't know what I'm going to do. We have just learned that this professor is non-Aryan. He has a quarter Jewish blood in his veins. I'm a good National Socialist. I believe that the Jews are the enemies, the potential destroyers, of my people and my culture, and I must do anything in my power to bring about the dismissal of this partly Jewish faculty member from our university."

Presently he added, "I've decided to do it."

It was quite simple, actually, because they had a system. My roommate just appeared outside the door of the classroom the next morning, and as the students arrived one by one to hear their customary lecture, he said, "I'm sorry, we've discovered that Professor So-and-So is non-Aryan. We cannot patronize his lecture." And whether out of fear or out of conviction—and for my present purpose it doesn't make too much difference which —not a single student went into that classroom that morning or the next or the next.

At the end of about a week, this professor had been boycotted in all of his courses and had no alternative; seeing the handwriting on the wall, understanding the method, knowing perfectly well what was happening, there was nothing left for him to do except quietly to disappear from Heidelberg. What happened to him after that I do not know.

The important thing that I wish to say, particularly to the large group of younger people whom I am so delighted to see here this morning, is to repeat what this roommate of mine said to me before he walked out the door. He said, "Not only do I love this man, and not only has he meant more to me than anyone else in this university, but we have a system here at Heidelberg under which, if a professor is dismissed or if for any reason his work is invalidated, all of the work that the students have done with that professor is likewise invalidated. We have to go back and do it all over again." Then he added, "In my case, this will mean that I will have to repeat anywhere from three to five semesters of my college course. But," he said firmly, "I have to do it."

And the four simple words with which he concluded his statement burned themselves indelibly upon my memory. He said, quite simply, "I believe this thing. *I believe this thing!*"

Now here was a diabolical faith. If there were time I could demonstrate that this particular delusion had many of the manifestations and characteristics of a religious belief. It was something on which people staked their lives. Distorted, antisocial, cruel, racist, nationalist, opportunistic—and yet it was a faith, a religion.

At that moment, I could not but ask myself and of course have had occasion in succeeding decades to ask myself: What is there in the hearts of our American young people in college, in the universities, or on out into the responsibilities of adulthood— facing the complexities and ambiguities of contemporary society —what is there that the rising generation really believes in, with a kind of passionate faith, backed by sacrificial action, comparable to that of this young Nazi student?

You might consider this a bizarre comparison. But I needn't remind you that our time is scarred by the presence of warring ideologies. Conflicting views of life have fastened their grip upon many in our society, and I do not single out any particular group. Against the background of this illustration of faith expressing itself in action, can there be any question as to whether there is a relationship between what one believes and what one does?

Are you not confronted daily with people who say that it makes no difference what you believe, it is what you do that counts? I should like to testify that this is a logical impossibility. Faith without manifestation in action is a contradiction in terms. In the last analysis, you are going to do with your life and in your life that which is most meaningful and gives a sense of direction to your life. It is meaning that motivates. What you do flows out of what you believe—even if you have not articulated that belief with full clarity.

The relation of belief to action is an issue as old as the life of man. In both concept and practice it has plagued every major religion and has been a continuing theme throughout the history of Christianity.

Among many of us there is a subtle assumption that faith and works are opposites which need to be reconciled. It is the Christian position that belief and action, far from being antinomies, are inseparable components of the religious life. Each is essential to the other.

"Faith without works is dead." It is an empty posturing, doomed to futility.

But works without faith is sterile. Action without a sense of its ultimate meaning is an exercise in frustration. James the Apostle was not downgrading faith. Faith was his point of departure—the accepted, the given of the Christian experience. Faith was the foundation of life—and it is so today.

Nor is this life of faith simply a personal crutch, a kind of inner assurance that helps me through as an individual. The kind of religion which confines itself to the salvation of one's own soul on the basis of faith and shows little concern for its application in human relations is a travesty on the Christian faith and a cop-out for the so-called believer. Christianity is faith lived out in community—the community of believers and the larger community of all God's children. It is difficult, if not impossible, to be a Christian by oneself.

The issue of faith and works is an issue in the life of our nation.

A concern of all right-thinking Americans is the state of faith of our people. To some, the issue is loss of religious certainty. To others, faith is associated with a wide range of values identified with our history and national mores which might or might not be religious in the Christian definition. But they are values which the Christian joins in affirming. To still others, the issue is not faith itself but its applications in life. It is the issue of integrity. This should be a concern of every citizen, from the high school student to the highest officials of the land.

Do all of us here, including your speaker of the morning, express our faith in action? If one believes one thing and does another, he simply does not believe that thing. If he believes it and does it, as the Heidelberg student did, his faith is at work. This is a very critical and hard test to put upon one's religion, but nothing less will suffice at a time like ours. The forces of competing faiths are too strong for us if we do not hold our faith deeply and apply it consistently.

For many of us—and I am sure for all of you here—the highest faith is the one which is manifested adequately only in Jesus Christ, who to us is the Supreme Revealer of God and of His will for men. He sent His Son so that men might see the perfect blend of faith and works.

I pray for you young people and for all in posts of responsibility, that you might get that grip on your faith that will give you the courage to act as our times demand. Courage is not a Christian monopoly. It is manifested by some whose faith is contrary to all for which Christ lived and died. Remember the Heidelberg student. He said, "I believe this thing," and he acted accordingly. We need a faith to live by, and we must live our faith. Faith and works are one.

Almighty God, our Father, especially in the presence here of those who carry such momentous responsibility for the life of our nation and the life of the world, grant to them and to every one of us that integrity of life which is represented by the oneness of faith and action. Grant us the power by thy Holy Spirit to discern thy will for us and to have the courage to do it. We pray in the name and for the sake of Jesus Christ, our divine Lord and Saviour. Amen.

## May 25, 1969

Prelude

Opening Remarks                          THE PRESIDENT

Doxology

Prayer        HIS EMINENCE TERENCE CARDINAL COOKE
                                   Archbishop of New York

Hymn                    *"Praise to the Lord, the Almighty"*

Anthem                                    Members of the
                              FOUNDRY CATHEDRAL CHOIR
                     *"God So Loved the World"* by John Stainer
                                     Director: Glenn Carow
                                   Organist: Beverly Carow

Sermon

Hymn                    *"Holy God, We Praise Thy Name"*

Benediction

Postlude

Singing this morning are members of the Foundry
Cathedral Choir from Foundry United Methodist
Church in Washington, D.C. Mr. Glenn Carow, who
has been organist and choir director at the church for
twenty-seven years, is directing the choir, and Mrs.
Carow will be accompanying on the organ.

# His Eminence Terence Cardinal Cooke

THE PRESIDENT: Forty-eight years ago, a baby boy was born to a very humble family in the Bronx in New York City. That boy grew up to be, first, a parish priest in his neighborhood, and just recently, in Rome, he became the youngest man in the history of his church to be a Prince of the Church. Mrs. Nixon and I have had the privilege of knowing our guest for many years—and particulary well for a year in New York. We knew him both for his warm, human qualities and for his inspirational leadership in the religious field. This house is very honored today to have, conducting our service, His Eminence Terence Cardinal Cooke.

CARDINAL COOKE: I am happy to join with you in this deeply moving ecumenical service and to have an opportunity to share with you some reflections on the great feast of Pentecost. On this occasion we pray for the brave members of the crew of Apollo 10 who are in the hands of the Lord as they move through space, advancing the frontiers of knowledge, understanding, and wisdom. Our thoughts are with them as they pierce the vastness of the universe and look upon the face of the earth. Our thoughts of Apollo 10, it seems to me, blend quite harmoniously with our reflections on Pentecost.

The Book of Wisdom stated the belief that "The Spirit of the Lord fills the world, is all-embracing, and knows every man's utterance." The Psalmist prayed, "Send forth Your Spirit, and they shall be created; and You shall renew the face of the earth."

And Jesus promised to send the Holy Spirit of God to his disciples. "The Paraclete, the Holy Spirit, whom the Father will send in my name, will teach you everything and remind you of all that I told you myself."

It is upon this *presence* and *activity* of the Spirit of God among us, in us, and through us, that I should like to meditate with you this morning: the Presence of the Spirit that is timeless, all-knowing, and all-embracing, the activity of the Spirit that is creative, renewing, and consoling.

So much of our attention is inevitably taken up these days with bad news, unhappiness, false ideals, shattered hopes. So often we are forced to think of the disunifying elements and the disruptive fragmentation in our society. It seems that we find little time and little encouragement to reflect upon the great facts and forces that unite us. The factors which unite mankind are far more fundamental than the factors which divide mankind. Yes, no matter what divides us, the things that unite us are greater and more important still—and we must be convinced of this. We are one family with God as Father of all; we are all brothers in His family. We are one in our requirement for the physical needs of life—food, clothing, and shelter; and we are united in the needs of our spirit. Each of us needs the food and union of the spirit found in art, music, and literature; each of us requires for the fullness of his humanity the clothing of virtuous living since without faith and hope and love, no one of us can lead a truly human life. And each of us knows how much his whole being calls out for peace and happiness.

We know how difficult and even how impossible it is for any one of us to achieve these needs—these goals—in a solitary way. The courageous man in space unquestionably has the right perspective when he looks down from above and sees one world. This—whether or not we always recognize it—is exactly what we are. We live in one world! We are united in our weaknesses; in sickness, suffering, death; in the social ills that plague us all. And

there can be no real and lasting progress toward the development
of any group of men without the simultaneous development of
all humanity in a true spirit of solidarity.

This is a great spiritual dimension of our life. All men *are* one
family—we have to say this to ourselves time and again, in the
face of whatever disunifying facts we see. We *are* one family—we
have to believe it, no matter how depressing or sensational the
day's events may be. We *are* one family—we have to hope and
work steadfastly for the strengthening of our family unity. Man
must meet man, nation must meet nation, as brothers and sisters,
as sons of God.

Today, we reflect together on our need for the Spirit of God
in achieving our unity fully as a family. The Spirit of the Lord fills
the world! It is all-embracing, and it can renew the face of the
earth. The Spirit of the Lord hovers over the whole world and
every man—to be a source of hope for all, to ignite the fire of love
in all, to unite all within itself.

We should ever marvel at the presence in ourselves of the
Spirit of the Lord which fills the whole world. We should give
thanks for the workings of that Spirit in each of us through the
years. We appreciate, of course, that this life of the Spirit in us
is difficult to analyze. We cannot set down all that the Spirit of
the Lord has caused in us during the years of our belief. God only
knows! Yet we firmly believe that His Spirit has been constantly
at work in us through mysterious, directly divine ways as well as
through human influences and human decisions. To the extent
that we have opened ourselves to the impulses of the divine
Spirit, we have become more human, more free, and more one
family in God.

The Spirit of the Lord, which fills the whole world and holds
all things in being and takes cognizance of every sound we utter,
has guided us through the years to make free decisions which
profoundly influence our own lives and the lives of many other
people. This is a fact of our belief—proved by our presence here

this morning. Our decisions have been moved and molded by the Spirit of God, and our decisions have also been free. It is a spiritual fact that has deep significance for every individual life. The Spirit of the Lord moves and directs each one of us and it is a great part, if not the whole, of our calling to do God's Will —to conform our personal decisions and personal histories with the decisions and living history of the Spirit within us—to think and live in the Spirit of the Lord.

The active presence of God's Spirit in each of us is a startling and almost overwhelming truth. Even the simplest statement of it causes us to wonder, and the wonder may well deepen our wisdom. Deep within us, we believers know well that we have been invited by the Spirit of the Lord to offer our hands, our hearts, and our wills to our heavenly Father for the continuance of His saving work for all mankind; to be His messengers of freedom and His instruments of peace; to bring to our brothers the joy of a fuller and more abundant life.

In a spiritual and a physical sense, no man is an island. We are not to live in this world for ourselves alone. No human soul is to be closed within itself but it is intended to be open to all mankind. God expects each of us to make a personal effort to renew and transform the world; to take up and purify all things; to regroup all things in a new and better order. And we know well that each of us is called by the Spirit to identify himself with our Almighty Father to ransom the time, to save our brothers.

This, too, is a great, startling, and almost overwhelming truth. It causes us to marvel; it makes us wonder at the greatness of our calling. At the same time, it makes us question our own fidelity to the Spirit of God which is present and active within us. Our own freely given fidelity, our openness to the Spirit, our conscious desire to do the works of the Spirit—how necessary this is. We are not thinking of an automatic process but of a free collaboration, fully divine and fully human, to which the believer must give his free and deliberate allegiance.

What are the works willed by the Spirit here and now in our beloved America in 1969? No one here this morning needs to be reminded of our nation's problems, of the many voices calling out—whether loudly or in muted tones—for salvation and the more abundant life, of the various forces that are weakening our national unity and often hampering our national purpose. War, hunger, racism, degrading poverty, inadequate housing, the threat of nuclear holocaust, the deprivation of freedom—these are matters which have our constant, urgent attention. Would it not be proper to suggest, as believer to believer, that, in working to meet these great and basic needs, the life and dynamism of the Spirit of God in each of us should also be given our constant, urgent attention. For, in all our planning, decision-making, implementation, and evaluation, we need the Spirit of God who *alone* fills the whole world.

How much and yet really how little we can do alone. We cannot succeed in strengthening the bonds that unite us—the Fatherhood of God, the brotherhood of man, our noble national ideals of true freedom and equal opportunity—without the creative help of the Spirit of the Lord, freely sought and accepted. We cannot achieve a realistic awareness of our need for one another, and a consciousness that we must be one in facing our problems, without the fire of love given by that Spirit.

St. Augustine phrased a practical norm that could be adopted by any believer: "I shall work as if everything depended on me; I shall pray as if everything depended on God." Here, in one sentence, is the mystery of divine-human cooperation and collaboration. And here too is a way in which a believer can proceed. In the days ahead, all of us shall work in a great variety of ways to build the common future of the human race. Naturally, we think first of the work of our President. We pray that the Spirit of the Lord will ever be with him and guide him in his countless burdens and responsibilities. We dedicate ourselves to work and pray with him, with each other, with faith in the future, and in the

Spirit of God which alone can truly "renew the face of the earth."
Working together, we shall more and more truly and fully become one family—and this is the very thing God our Father
intended us to be.

As members of one human family, it is God's wish that we share
the deep joy, the true peace, the real contentment of living as His
children on His good earth. And it is only by our cooperation
with the power of the Spirit that this can be accomplished. There
is no other way! Today and every day in the future, we need the
Spirit of the Lord which "fills the world, is all-embracing, and
knows every man's utterance." Today and every day in the future,
*together* we need to pray, "Send forth Your Spirit, and they shall
be created; and You shall renew the face of the earth."

# June 15, 1969

Prelude

Opening Remarks THE PRESIDENT

Doxology

Prayer THE REVEREND DR. NORMAN VINCENT PEALE
The Marble Collegiate Church, New York City

Hymn *"Holy, Holy, Holy! Lord God Almighty"*

Anthem THE MEN'S CHOIR OF DOUGLAS
MEMORIAL COMMUNITY CHURCH
*"The Spirit of the Lord"* by Everett Titcomb
Director: Mr. Spencer Hammond

Sermon

Hymn *"Faith of Our Fathers"*

Benediction

Postlude

The choir this morning includes members of the adult choir of the Douglas Memorial Community Church. This all-male group, organized for the past seven years, performs for special services at the Church and for various community affairs. Directing the choir is Mr. Spencer Hammond.

# The Reverend Dr. Norman Vincent Peale

THE PRESIDENT: Since we first met Dr. Peale twenty-five years ago at the end of World War II, we have had the opportunity, my wife and I and later our daughters, to hear him on many occasions. During the four years we lived in New York, we regularly attended his church. We not only knew him from his sermons, but we also had the privilege of knowing him personally and knowing Mrs. Peale as well, and their family. I can say sincerely that never have we heard him, over those many times, that he has not been a great inspiration to us. This house is privileged to have, conducting our Worship Service this morning, Dr. Norman Vincent Peale.

DR. PEALE: Almighty God, our heavenly Father, help everyone here this day to sense thy presence. May the world, with all of its confusion and its demands, retreat for these moments, and may we be with thee in the peace of eternity. "Thou wilt keep him in perfect peace, whose mind is stayed on thee." "Come unto me, all ye that labour and are heavy laden, and I will give you rest." "Peace I give unto you: not as the world giveth, give I unto you. Let not your heart be troubled, neither let it be afraid."

We invoke thy divine blessing upon this service, upon this house, upon the President of the United States and his family and all those who, with him, are charged with the government of this blessed land. God bless America and all of its people. Bring peace in our time, O Lord. May all of the children of men have a new sense of thy guidance. Through Jesus Christ our Lord. Amen.

It is indeed an honor to be here this morning to conduct a service of worship at the invitation of the President of the United States. I must say that we miss President and Mrs. Nixon in New York, particularly at the Marble Collegiate Church, where they attended so many times in the years gone by. And I will have to admit publicly that he is the one and only member of my congregation whom I helped to move to another city. It is also a privilege to see here this morning David and Julie, one of the most wonderful young couples I ever had the pleasure of uniting in matrimony—and their lovely sister, Tricia.

This is Father's Day, and we honor our fathers and express our love for them. It's a privilege to preach in the presence of the first father of the nation. I don't know whether he's ever been called that before or not, but this is what he is: father to his children, and in a deep sense, presiding from this historic and venerated place, the father of his people.

Being a father myself, I know something about the problems that a father possesses: and I wish to speak to you for just a few moments on this phenomenon known as a problem. I think people generally take a dim view of it. They assume that there is something inherently bad about a problem. And they believe that life would be simply wonderful if either they had fewer problems or easier problems, or, better still, no problems whatsoever.

Actually, would we be better off with fewer or easier or no problems at all? And is a problem inherently a bad thing? May it not, on the contrary, be a very good thing? Let me answer my own question by telling you of an incident.

I was walking down Fifth Avenue in New York City not long ago when I saw approaching me a friend of mine by the name of George. It was obvious from George's disconsolate and melancholy demeanor that he wasn't what you might call filled to overflowing with the ecstasy and exuberance of human existence. Which is a rather fancy way of saying that he was really dragging bottom; he was low. This excited my natural sympathy, so I asked him, "How are you, George?" Well, now, when you get right down to it, that was nothing but a routine inquiry. But George took it seriously and for fifteen minutes enlightened me meticulously on how badly he felt. And the more he talked, the worse I felt. Finally I asked, "George, what seems to be the difficulty?"

This really set him off. "Oh," he said, "it's these problems. Problems, nothing but problems, I am fed up with problems." And he got so exercised about the matter that he quite forgot whom he was talking to, and he began to castigate these problems vitriolically, using in the process thereof, I am sad to relate, a great many theological terms—though he didn't put them together in a theological manner, I assure you. But I knew what he meant, all right, for he had what the supererudite call the "power to communicate."

"Well," I said, "George, I certainly would like to help you if I can. What can I do for you?"

"Oh," he said, "get me rid of these problems."

I said, "Do you mean that? All of them?"

"Yes," he said, "all of them."

Always being willing to oblige as best I can, I said, "George, the other day I was up in the northern part of New York City in the Bronx on professional business in a place where the head man told me there were some one hundred thousand people and not a single one of them had a problem."

The first enthusiasm I saw in George flashed up in his eyes and suffused his countenance as he said, "Boy, that's for me. Lead me to this place."

I said, "All right, you asked for it. It's Woodlawn Cemetery in the Bronx." And this is a fact. Nobody in Woodlawn has a problem. They couldn't care less for what we will see on television tonight or read in tomorrow morning's newspapers. They have no problems at all. But . . . they are dead.

It therefore follows, I believe, in logical sequence, that problems constitute a sign of life. Indeed, I would go so far as to say that the more problems you have, the more alive you are. The man who has, let's say, ten good old tough, man-sized problems is twice as alive as the poor miserable, apathetic character who only has five problems.

Problems are written into the constitution of the universe. When God made this world the way it is, He inserted in it the phenomenon of a problem. For what purpose? Well, I can only guess at what was in His mind, but what I know about Him would indicate that what He wants to do is to make real people out of us. For you never grow strong without resistance and struggle; and problems are part of that creative phenomenon known as struggle. So I call to your attention on this Father's Day that problems are good for individuals and for a great, developing nation. As the nation solves its problems it will produce a strong people.

What, then, are a few suggestions for handling a problem? There's a text in Philippians, 4:13, which comes to my mind: "I can do all things through Christ which strengtheneth me." One of the modern interpretations of that passage is this: "I have the strength to face all conditions by the power that Christ gives me." With that as a background, I suggest three principles for handling a problem: First, the "in-spite-of" principle; second, the "relentless-pressure" principle; and third, the "as-if" principle.

What do we mean by the "in-spite-of" principle? It means that when you are fortified by an inward consciousness of God and the Lord Jesus Christ you look at your problems and say, "Yes, I see you. You are very formidable, you are very complicated, but in spite of what you are, I have what it takes to handle you." And we do, too, if we trust God and if we think. And the two are one and inseparable, because real trust in God is the profoundest thinking known to man.

I have a humble little illustration about a boy fifteen years old. He was an unusual boy. The summer vacation came along, and he said to his father, "Dad, I don't want to sponge on you all summer; I want a job." The father, when he recovered from his surprise, encouraged him in this. So he read the want ads, and found a job offer which said that applicants should show up the next morning at eight o'clock. He was there. But so were twenty other boys, lining up, facing the secretary of the man who was doing the hiring.

The average boy might have looked at these other kids and said, "They're all good boys. Any one of them will get the job. I at least tried—I've done the best I can and at the twenty-first position in line there's no opportunity whatsoever." But this boy believed in the "in-spite-of" principle. So he thought, really thought. And if you really think, you can get a solution to any problem that will ever face you.

An inspiration came to him. He took a piece of paper; he wrote something quickly on it. He walked over to the secretary of the man doing the hiring, a rather formidable-looking girl. He bowed politely to her and said, "Miss, this message is of the utmost importance to your boss. Please deliver it to him immediately."

She looked at the message and she smiled. She immediately rose, went into the office, laid the message on the desk of the boss, who read it and laughed out loud, for this is what it said: "Dear Sir, I am the 21st kid in line; don't do anything until you see me." It would seem that all of us who are believers in God and His sustaining power and guidance should know that we, like that young man, have the inner capacity to handle any problem. He made use of the "in-spite-of" principle. That is one great formula for solving problems.

The second is the "relentless-pressure" principle. Obviously I have to give these very sketchily because of the limitations of time, but it's a simple thing. Nobody ever succeeded at anything in this life who didn't keep everlastingly at it. If it won't respond one way, you come at it another way. You attack it from before and behind, from above and below—any way that there's the slightest opportunity to gain the objective and the result. If you "can do all things through Christ," who gives you the strength, then if your goal and objective are right, reached in prayer and meditation and under the guidance of God, you have just got to keep at it until you gain a victory.

Not long ago, I visited Chartwell in Kent, Churchill's old home. While there, somebody told me about the time Churchill was invited by the headmaster of his old school to come and give a talk. The headmaster told the boys that an immortal utterance was going to be made, one that they would remember until their dying days, and he had them properly conditioned for it. At the appointed time, the great man came. He stood before them: he pulled his glasses down over his nose, as was his custom, and looked them over—bright young boys' faces, and he went back into the long reaches of memory to when he as a little boy sat out there on one of those same benches, in which students have carved their initials for six hundred years. And he saw this little fellow who was shy and who stuttered. He had great thoughts even then, but the words piled up under his tongue, yet, in time, he spoke and wrote the greatest English of our era. And a dead silence fell. Finally he spoke this immortal message: "Never give in, never, never, never, never!" That was the essence of his speech. And a great, profound, philosophical truth had been uttered—the "relentless-pressure" principle.

"I have the strength to face all conditions. . . ."

I believe, this, friends. I am positive of it. "I have the strength to face all conditions. . . ." Through my own strength and wisdom? Why of course not. But "by the power that Christ gives me."

And principle number three is the "as-if" principle. This principle was first announced by the late Professor William James, who at one time taught, so I understand, anatomy, psychology, and philosophy at Harvard—which meant, you might say, that he was professor of body, mind, and soul. He was the father of

American philosophical psychology, one of the great men of our history.

He announced the "as-if" principle. It means that if you have one condition, you are dissatisfied with it, and you want another which is greater, you act *as if* you had the other, and all the forces of your nature conspire to produce this condition in fact. If you are full of fear and anxiety, for example, and you want to be full of courage and confidence, you try—feebly at first—but you try to act as if you had those virtues. And something in the construction of your nature brings it realistically into fact.

Lots of people have lots of problems. I have a letter here from a little girl—naturally I shall not give you her name or where she lives, but just say she is a very young girl. This is her letter: "Dear Dr. Peale, I have this problem that I would like you to send me some booklets on. My mother is on dope and I'm living with my grandmother. My mother never married. We don't get to see her very often, that is, my sister and I. And could you put her on your prayer list? I go to church every Sunday. I'm only nine years old so I don't really understand."

All the pathos of human life is in this plea of a little girl for a better life. She wants me to pray for her mother. She wants to know how she can overcome these problems. What did I write her? I told her how deeply I felt her problems and how proud I was of her strength in facing up to them. Then I wrote, "Honey, you just try to get even more acquainted with Jesus Christ, because he will help you to handle any condition." And I described as best I could to her the "as-if" principle. "Just act 'as if' you're going to have a great life. And I can assure you that you will."

Our heavenly Father, bless this message to our hearts, and help us to live with thee and with thy Son Jesus Christ so faithfully that strength and power and peace and goodness will fill our hearts forever. Through Jesus Christ our Lord. Amen.

# *June 29, 1969*

Prelude

Opening Remarks            THE PRESIDENT

Doxology

Prayer            DR. LOUIS FINKELSTEIN
Chancellor, The Jewish Theological
Seminary of America
New York City

Hymn            *"We Gather Together"*

Anthem            Members of the Christ Lutheran
Church Choir
*"Now God Be Praised In Heav'n Above"*
by MELCHIOR VULPIUS
Director: MR. GEOFFREY SIMON

Sermon

Hymn            *"O God, Our Help in Ages Past"*

Benediction

Postlude

The choir this morning represents a long established
Washington church, Christ Lutheran Church, which
was founded over seventy-five years ago. During worship services at Christ Lutheran, the choir performs
anthems ranging from compositions of the eleventh
century to present-day arrangements. Mr. Geoffrey
Simon is directing the choir.

# Dr. Louis Finkelstein

THE PRESIDENT: We are greatly pleased this morning to have with us one of the most distinguished religious leaders of our time. I can say that because he has been one of the few religious leaders to appear on the cover of *Time* Magazine, and also because he has served three presidents in various capacities—President Roosevelt, President Kennedy, and President Eisenhower. In 1957, he participated in the presidential inaugural ceremonies, offering one of the prayers at the second Eisenhower-Nixon inauguration. Since the year 1951 he has been Chancellor of The Jewish Theological Seminary of America in New York City. And he is, of course, one of America's most outstanding authors in the religious field. This house is honored by the presence of Dr. Louis Finklestein, who will conduct our Worship Service this morning.

DR. FINKLESTEIN: In our ritual, when one sees the Head of State, one has to thank God for that privilege; therefore, before doing anything else, I will recite the blessing which I'm required to recite on this occasion: Blessed art thou, O Lord our God, King of the Universe, who has given human beings part of thy glory.

In 1957, when privileged to offer the invocation at the second inaugural of President Dwight David Eisenhower, I could not foresee, of course, that twelve years later his successor, linked also to him by family ties, would invite me to participate with him in a worship service. Yet, the same prayer now offered for the thirty-seventh President and Vice-President retains its ancient inspiration:

God of our fathers, grant Richard Milhous Nixon and Spiro Agnew the blessings sought of thee for all mankind by the great scholar Rab sixteen centuries ago in Babylonia. Give them long life, a life of peace, a life of happiness, and, above all, a life which may prove a blessing to mankind. Do thou fulfill in their days, and in ours, thy promise to the Prophets, that thou wilt cause the spirit of thee to enter the hearts of all thy creatures, so that mankind may become one society dedicated with a complete heart to perform thy will. May wickedness be silenced; may the rule of arrogance vanish and thou alone reign over all. Our Father and our King, may our time be ripe for thine own intervention, as of yore, to inspire us to obey thee; and may all mankind join us in thy service, for their own sake and for the sake of thy holy name. Amen.

Mr. President, Mrs. Nixon, Mr. Chief Justice, Mrs. Burger, ladies and gentlemen:

One is frequently asked to define the American way of life which we struggle so hard to protect and develop. No good definition describes this way of life to those who have not experienced it. But what cannot be described in words sometimes can be described in scenes. There are scenes distinctive of America which scarcely occur anywhere else, even in the free world. One of them is taking place in this room today. Here are gathered leaders of our nation, among others, to pray together, uniting across differences of background and doctrine before the throne of the Judge of us all.

In the face of crises which seemed insoluble, my great predecessor, Solomon Schechter, used to say, "You must leave a little bit to God." He did not mean that we are free from responsibility to alleviate human agony. He tried to express in a simple aphorism the insight of a sage who flourished in Judea at the end of the first century, who taught his disciples: "You are not obliged to complete the task—that is, the task of making the world a better place to live in—but neither are you free to desist from it." Or, as he put it on another occasion, "Do not flinch from a task which by its nature can never be completed."

How little the mightiest of us can really hope to achieve and how much we have to leave to God! How much we can do with His help, and how little can we hope to do without it! And how secure we must be that, no matter what follies we may commit, ultimately He will save us from the worst results of our errors.

After all, here we are, all sentient human beings, yet all descended from primeval bits of protoplasm, themselves incredibly combined from inanimate bits of protein. Perhaps it took some three billion years for these unicellular animals to become human beings. But I think we will all admit that three billion years is not a long time for a bacterium to graduate into manhood.

The primeval cells had no notion of purpose. Neither did the earthworms which, in the course of eons, began the adventurous road to mammals, primates, and humans, impelled by a force which still eludes our understanding. Heirs to all their strengths and weaknesses, we are their direct descendants, thinking, writing, speaking, speculating, planning, and even, from time to time, communing with God Himself. Having brought us so far, is it possible to believe that this Cosmic Force will desert us, simply because we are now sentient human beings rather than unicellular bacteria and amoebae? Instead, must we not rationally assume that the divine Power that brought us from such humble beginnings is still with us and will lead us onward to even greater heights? As men we, alone among animal species, have the power to envisage the future and to choose. We can act wisely and we can also act foolishly.

The machinery which constantly saves us from our sins of omission and commission appears most clearly perhaps in the life of society. American history has many examples of this divine intervention in human affairs. It is astonishing that so few understand it as a chronicle of miracles no less extraordinary than those recorded in Scripture. American history could properly be told in the style of the Book of Judges. Whenever some self-induced danger threatened, leaders were sent to us to save our country for its intended destiny of service. Where would we be today, where could the hope of the free world be, where would be the future of civilization, if in the crisis of the beginning of this Republic it had lacked such redoubtable figures as Benjamin Franklin, George Washington, Thomas Jefferson, and Alexander Hamilton, to mention only a few?

That great tragedy, the War Between the States, arose from many failures of human judgment. But, remarkably, the compassion and wisdom of Abraham Lincoln became available just when they were essential. Where would the Western world, including our own country, have been today if Winston Churchill had not, through what at the time seemed mere chance, been the articulate leader of Britain, standing alone between impending barbarism and civilization, guarding us until we could protect ourselves and everyone else?

Miracles occur not only in historical crises; they are happening every day, all the time, for each of us. Everyone in this room is alive due to uncounted miracles as commonplace as the rising and setting of the sun.

A student at our seminary once asked me whether I really believed in the miracle of the Israelites crossing the Red Sea. Actually, properly interpreted, Scripture says that they crossed not "the Red Sea" but a "sea of reeds," possibly a small body of water. But as Exodus relates the story, it is about as remarkable as the American defeat of the Japanese Navy at Midway, which was a turning point in the Second World War.

I could have mentioned this to the doubting student. I could also have mentioned very well-authenticated miracles, like the American Constitution, a document drawn up by human beings almost two hundred years ago, but which seems to many of us inspired by almost divine wisdom, and by which we have been guided for all these generations—and which has become a model for many other nations. I could have mentioned the miracle of

the Second World War, when in 1940 the Allies seemed hope-
lessly defeated and yet in 1945 they emerged victorious. As the
student was, himself, a refugee from oppression who had fled to
Jerusalem before he came to the United States, I could have come
very near to his own experience by speaking of the miracle of the
emergence of the State of Israel—an event without parallel in the
annals of mankind.

I must admit that these answers occurred to me after I was on
my way home from the seminary. My reply to him was different.
I said I was not present at the crossing of the Red Sea, so I could
not add my testimony to what is found in Scripture. I certainly
believe in miracles. And one of the miracles in which I believe
most firmly is that you and I exist, despite the fact that our lives
are in dire jeopardy every moment, and would cease if everything
depended on our conscious thought.

I recommended that the student read a book by Walter B.
Cannon, formerly a professor of physiology at Harvard University, a book called *The Wisdom of the Body*. It is a learned and wise
work, though doubtless, since its appearance many years ago,
others have superseded some of its facts. Professor Cannon
shows what miracles go on at every moment within us: what
ingenuity beyond the power of the cleverest engineer enables the
eye to see, the ear to hear, the hand to touch, and above all, the
mind to think. How strange it is that no matter how much liquid
we drink, our blood never becomes diluted but is kept in proper
balance. How incredible that the single cell from which each one
of us developed should carry the potential of every quality des-
tined to appear in us in its proper season; that the cells multiply-
ing from this original one should have separate functions, one
becoming a brain cell, one becoming a red corpuscle, one becoming a bone cell—and all without error or confusion.

Of course, sometimes the miraculous is obscured. There is
much that is imperfect in human life, both individual and commu-
nal; that, I think, is what we should expect. Why should it be

otherwise? What needs explanation is how so much happens to be right, even though the world and each of its parts is far too complex for the wisest of us to comprehend. Once more, as Solomon Schechter said, "You must leave a little bit to God." He has been, He is, He will be. We must try to do what we can, and it is a great privilege for us when we do well and find the path of the right. At such times we are cooperating with God; to use the rabbinical expression, "We are His partners." And He is working through us and with us.

Happy is he who, like Lincoln, is privileged to save his fellows from the evils threatened by their own misdeeds—he whose life represents an intervention of the Divine into human affairs. The faith that all will be well in the last analysis enables us to be steadfast in peril and modest in success, to escape foolish hand-wringing and paralysis and at the same time thoughtless panic and fear. Again, if you will permit me, as Schechter said, "We must leave a little bit to God."

I hope it is not presumptuous of me, a guest of the President of the United States, to pray that the future historian, looking back on our generation, may say, as I said of Lincoln, that in a period of great trials and great tribulations, the finger of God pointed to Richard Milhous Nixon, giving him the vision and the wisdom to save the world and civilization; and also to open the way for our country to realize the good that the twentieth century offers mankind.

And now, with your permission, I would like to conclude with the ancient verse traditionally closing the daily Jewish worship service, called in Hebrew *Adon Olam*:

> Lord of the world, the King Supreme,
> Ere ought was formed, He reigned alone.
> When by His will, all things were wrought,
> Then was His sovereign name made known.

And when in time all things shall cease,
He still shall reign in majesty.
He was, He is. He shall remain
All-glorious eternally.

Incomparable, unique is He,
No other can His Oneness share.
Without beginning, without end,
Dominion's might is His to bear.

He is my living God who saves,
My Rock when grief or trials befall,
My Banner and my Refuge strong,
My bounteous Portion when I call.

My soul I give unto His care,
Asleep, awake, for He is near,
And with my soul, my body too,
God is with me, I have no fear.

# July 13, 1969

Prelude

Opening Remarks            THE PRESIDENT

Doxology

Prayer     THE REVEREND PAUL H. A. NOREN, D.D.
Senior Pastor, Mount Olivet Lutheran Church,
Minneapolis, Minnesota

Hymn                     *"Faith of Our Fathers"*

Anthem            SANCTUARY CHOIR OF BOYS
Shrine of the Most Blessed Sacrament
*"With a Voice of Singing"* by Martin Shaw
Lawrence Sears, choir master
Lawrence Redmond, organist

Sermon                "The Great Adventure"

Hymn               *"This Is My Father's World"*

Benediction

Postlude

The Sanctuary Choir of Boys from the Shrine of the
Most Blessed Sacrament in Washington, D.C., was
founded in 1955. In 1960 the choir sang in the presence of President Eisenhower at the Christmas Tree
Lighting Ceremonies, and in 1961 they performed for
Pope John XXIII. The choir is composed of boys
ranging from age seven through twelve.

# The Reverend Dr. Paul H. A. Noren

THE PRESIDENT: Mr. Chief Justice and all of our very distinguished guests this morning: We are most honored to have with us today a man who was born in Minnesota, was educated there, for the past fifteen years has been in Denver, Colorado, and now has returned to his home in Minnesota where he is the senior pastor of Mount Olivet Lutheran Church in Minneapolis. It is, by the way, the largest Lutheran Church in the United States and very possibly the largest in the world. It is with genuine pleasure that I introduce Dr. Paul Noren, who will conduct our Worship Service.

DR. NOREN: O God of a million, million wonders, Creator of the universe, Redeemer of our lives, we come before thee in this sacred moment of prayer. We come in penitence, our Father. Forgive us when we have blustered and blundered. Forgive us our sometime escapes. We have been tempted to run from need and from hurt and from things that we have not understood. We come to thee in petition. We ask thy divine help in the girding of our space pioneers,* who with thy protection will soon make footprints on the moon. Give them steadiness under strain, we pray.

We pray also for our President. And while we cannot know personally the intensity of concern that rests upon his heart as he faces issues of world and domestic problems, we can and do ask that his hand may be strengthened and his spirit encouraged. Attend his visits in the Pacific,

*[Space ship Apollo 11 departed for the moon on July 16, 1969, to put the first men on the moon on July 20, 1969.]

71

in Asia, and in Europe with thy blessing, and keep him for the yet-to-be-accomplished missions of the future.

We come to thee in commitment, for we are here in trust, in trust to thee, O God, in trust to those whom we serve, in trust to those who have sacrificed for us, in trust to those who have helped prepare us for our place in life. Because we are here in trust, O God, grant that we may prove faithful and guide us, we pray, in life's continuing adventure. In the name of Christ we pray. Amen.

Mr. President, Mrs. Nixon, distinguished friends all: I want to thank you for your kind words, Mr. President, and for the privilege of being here this morning and sharing in this great experience; not least, to have had the pleasure of hearing these fine boys of the Sanctuary Choir of Boys of Washington—examples, I am sure, of the kind of youth that is coming up in America. With the kind of spirit they represent, we can be very hopeful of the tomorrows of our nation.

I hope that I may speak with you for just a few moments this morning on the topic, "The Great Adventure." Of all the ideas that stir the imagination and quicken the pulse of mankind, surely the word "adventure" is one that does this in a very significant way.

Something within us responds to great challenge. That recent attempt of a new 18-foot world mark by Bob Seagren had all of us going over the bar with him only to feel the frustration of his narrow miss. We are excited by the feats of our Frank Howards and Reggie Jacksons and Harmon Killebrews as they batter fences and hitting marks.

Within our common heritage are some superlative adventures. Let me speak of a Noah who with his sons built an ark without a sea on which to launch it—and heard the taunts and insults of those who would not believe that their world was in danger of God's judgment. And yet, they didn't take time off to run to their analyst to have their delusions examined. They were on an adventure for God. Or remember Abraham who was called to go out to a place which he was to receive as an inheritance, "and he went out, not knowing where he was to go." That, too, was a remarkable adventure. Recall the adventure of Moses in leading out of bondage the children of Israel. What a leader he was! His people had been serfs—but they refused to live in a slave-complex. The exciting climax of this episode finds the people of God under Caleb and Joshua watching the fingers of dawn give the promise of a new day as they marched around the ramparts of Jericho seven times and the walls came tumbling down!

We remember with gratitude the adventure of that One Perfect Life who saw the battle of the spirit squared at the place called Calvary, and who, through his sacrifice, has made possible the finest values for our lives here—and opened the gates to eternal life.

We can move on to the Early Church and recall the brave exploits of men so convinced of the Gospel they had received that they covered their world with its message, willing to give their lives for it!

We miss something really big when we restrict the Holy Spirit's activity to the pages of the Bible and conclude that His Activity ends with the last page of the New Testament. It is my belief that the continuing exploits of the Church have been within God's guidance. I do believe that God is the God of history—that He not only knows what is taking place but that His hand is active now as the prophets and Apostles saw Him active in Bible days.

So—we believe that we might add to the daring exploits of the heroes of the Bible—the explorations of medieval history and the adventure of Columbus when he discovered the New World and of the Pilgrim forefathers who came to our shores drawing up their Mayflower Compact which began, "In the Name of God. Amen."

Nor can we forget to place into this focus the importance of the processes of government. Some people would like to divorce this

whole function from divine concern—separating as we do so
easily the secular (as we call it) from the sacred. But I believe that
government is within the divine providence and direction. And
so, Mr. President, we join with many others around the world in
the prayer that your coming adventure in the Pacific, in Asia, and
in Europe may be successfully consummated—and that we shall
be that much closer to peace and world understanding because
of your dedicated involvement!

But let us not forget the adventures born of human curiosity.
This intriguing reach of the human mind and spirit after the yet
unknown and still not accomplished cannot be excluded—either
from our thought or from the reality of God's concern. For as
long as we have been looking at the night sky we have wondered
about the moon. Someone suggests that this has been for a period of fifty thousand years. Now we stand on the very threshold
of placing our footprints upon this heavenly body. Wrote Arthur
J. Snider (*Chicago Daily News*) in a release last week: "They may
look back and describe the moon landing as a Kitty Hawk affair,
but this generation will be forever acclaimed in the history books
as having achieved the greatest adventure in human history."

Now—that's quite a statement. It was actually in reading this
account that I arrived at my topic for this morning, "The Great
Adventure." I am heartily in accord with our space venture. The
very nature of the human mind and spirit with which we have
been endowed by God requires it. I should have to say that
among the half dozen greatest thrills I have experienced would
have to be the Christmas journey to the moon and the simple but
dramatic reading of the Creation Story by our spacemen!

Perhaps life's great adventure will be found in something con-
siderably simpler than a moon shot. May I give you a brief reminder of Naaman in the Old Testament (II Kings 5:1–15). He
was a great Syrian general, enjoyed the high favor of the king—
but he was a leper. A little maid of Israel—carried off by the
Syrians in one of their raids and a servant of Naaman's wife—said

one day, "I wish that my lord would see the prophet who is in Samaria. He would cure him of his leprosy." So the matter was arranged after protocol and influence had been properly arrived at, and yet with all of the friendly gestures that had been made —war almost broke out over such a simple incident (the ways of diplomacy have never been easy). But finally Naaman came to the house of Elisha, the prophet. But Elisha didn't show himself. Instead, he sent a servant to tell Naaman to go and wash in the Jordan seven times and he would be cured. Imagine! A famous general came and the prophet didn't even show himself. And the Syrian general wondered why he should bathe in the dirty waters of the Jordan. Weren't the Syrian rivers just as therapeutic? So Naaman stalked away in rage.

But now Naaman's servants took hold of him and said, "Listen, if the prophet had commanded you to do some great thing, wouldn't you have done it?" This was enough to cool the insult and Naaman dipped himself in the waters of the Jordan and was made whole from his leprosy!

We are tempted to think that the greatest adventures of all are those that bring forth the adrenalin—the daring, dramatic things. "If the prophet had commanded you to do some *great thing*, wouldn't you have done it?" Obviously!

Isn't life made up of many little things—all kinds and colors of thread that are woven into the tapestry of life—by faith?

What of the many little things we so easily take for granted— the acts of quiet heroism that never reach the front pages of our newspapers—the acts of integrity that go to make the fabric of greatness in our way of life, the faithful doing of a million small operations by tens of thousands of people that make successful a space flight—or the administration of a government?

And the greatest adventure of all—the quiet saying of "Yes!" to God for our salvation and in becoming a part of the "all things new" that is promised in Jesus Christ! Amen.

## *July 20, 1969*

Prelude

Opening Remarks                          THE PRESIDENT

Doxology

Prayer                          SENATOR MARK HATFIELD

Hymn                                  *"Navy Hymn"*

Reading from *Genesis*          COL. FRANK BORMAN,
                                            USAF
                          Commander, Apollo VIII

Sermon                          DR. PAUL S. SMITH
                  President of Whittier College
                          Whittier, California
              Member of the Society of Friends

Hymn                  *"O God, Our Help in Ages Past"*

Benediction                  CONGRESSMAN JOHN H.
                                  BUCHANAN, JR.

Postlude

# Dr. Paul S. Smith

THE PRESIDENT: The Vice President, the Chief Justice, members of the Cabinet, members of the Congress, and all of our distinguished guests this morning:

This is an historic day, as we all know, the day when man will first set foot on the moon. And on this occasion we have, participating in our worship service, three whose names are well known to everybody in this room and one other notable gentleman whom I shall introduce to you in a moment. The three are Senator Hatfield from the State of Oregon, a distinguished lay leader throughout the United States and a member of the Senate Prayer Group; from the House of Representatives, Congressman John Buchanan, an ordained Baptist minister and a member of the House Prayer Group; and Colonel Frank Borman, who needs no introduction.

I should tell you what happened to Colonel Borman recently, in order to introduce the fourth member of the group, who will be conducting our service. On June 7 of this year, Frank Borman delivered the commencement address at Whittier College and received an honorary degree. (Just thirty-five years earlier, I got a degree from Whittier College the hard way.) The man who presented the honorary degree to Frank Borman was Dr. Paul Smith, the president of Whittier College. Thirty-five years before, he was a professor of history and professor of government at Whittier. Of all the fine teachers I had—and there were many in my life—Dr. Paul Smith was the man who most inspired

77

me, and I am very proud that today he is here to conduct this
Worship Service. He, incidentally, is the first member of the
Society of Friends to be present at one of these Worship Services
in this capacity.

SENATOR HATFIELD: Our Father, we marvel at three brave space pioneers
as they prepare for a landing on the moon. From the depths of our
hearts, we pray for the safe return of Neil Armstrong, Edwin Aldrin, and
Michael Collins. Sustain their wives, their children, and families during
these anxious days. We are grateful for the thousands of support person-
nel who literally are their brothers' keepers. Excite our imagination to
transfer this genius of cooperation and spirit of teamwork to our many
other needs, lest our success on the moon mock our failures on the
earth. Even as our astronauts go to the moon in the name of peace, our
world aches from the pain of wars. We perfect the means for destroying
human life and then believe we have found security.

May the nations trust not in the power of their arms, but in the Prince
of Peace, thy Son. O God, grant us deliverance from the rhetoric of
peace when we personally are not willing to do things which make for
peace: to love, to forgive, to use wisely all gifts and resources for the
good of mankind; and to permit the invasion of the Holy Spirit into the
lives of each of us—that it may be reflected in our homes between
husbands and wives, between children and parents, and in commerce
between management and labor, between citizen and government and
among all races of men.

O Lord, keep us mindful that technical success does not necessarily
produce wisdom. We pray for wisdom for our President and all who
govern this nation. The true wisdom is found in Scripture and is described by St. James as the wisdom that comes from God, is utterly pure,
then peace-loving, considerate, open to reason, rich in mercy and kindly
actions, with no breath of favoritism or hint of hypocrisy. And the wise
are the peacemakers who go on quietly sowing for a harvest of righteousness in other people and in themselves. We pray for this in the name of
thy Son, our Saviour Jesus Christ. Amen.

DR. SMITH: The President's kind remarks this morning will indicate to you how fortunate it was for me that I moved from a

Midwestern state for a professional life in the State of California. And I may say in passing that the most valid test of how good education is, comes about when the pupil far outdistances the teacher. The President may not know, however, that as an undergraduate at Earlham, I earned my way in part as an itinerant minister in the Indiana Yearly Meeting of Friends. But never in my most evangelistic moments as a birthright Quaker did I see myself as standing in the presence of the mighty to proclaim the Word.

Nor am I a wandering prophet. I am here by gracious invitation, with the general directive to concern myself with the historical import of the moon landing and its relation to world peace. Because of my profession and birthright, I could scarcely have spoken otherwise and shall therefore entitle my sermonette "Reaching for the Moon."

For centuries, man has used that expression, literally and figuratively, to describe an essentially human characteristic which paradoxically is at once the most infantile and mature capability to make him what he is. In the fond groping of the cradled child, we smile upon the act with tender commiseration. In the fantastic insight of our great scientists and philosophers, we behold with awe man's ability to find out the combination of God's most secret locks.

For most of us, however, we must confess that maturation is a process of capitulation. We gradually resign ourselves to successive recognition of goals that are beyond our reach. For most of us, life acquires a network of enveloping guidelines that surround us with conventional limitations. It is the poet, then, the artist poet, fancy's child, who alone can find it in the heart to say that man's reach should exceed the routine, the commonplace, for what else is a heaven for? There would seem to be a certain spark of artistry in us all until it is snuffed out in the stuffy atmosphere of the worldly network. And even the artist comes to recognize the limitations of his medium, be it paint, wood, stone, bronze, sound, or language.

The philosopher is a somewhat different case. His medium is his own artifact, language, and in a sense language is not subject to the limitations of the other media I have mentioned. As the poet works his wonders with word-born images, so the philosopher applies his magic to word-fabricated abstractions. We can take the terms "knowing," "powerful," and "present" and place before them the prefix "all" and "ever," and then can take the word "God," and with the word "is" make the sentence, "God is all-knowing, all-powerful, and ever-present."

As a student of history and government, I am profoundly conscious at this moment in the history of mankind that most of this select gathering are responsible members of the oldest political democracy in history. And I am struck by the irony of the fact that the context is one in which the term "light-year" is becoming a household word. But I must remind you, ladies and gentlemen, that this democracy has yet to celebrate its second centennial. It is indeed younger than the city of San Diego.

I am further mindful that the Charter and the later Constitution of this most stable of political democracies were the inspired work of philosophers who worked with such magic abstractions as "all," "inalienable," "right," "liberty," and "justice"; and that many of them, in *their* context, were deliberately subscribing to the inalienable right of revolution while in the very act of composing the verbal guidelines for the entertainment of law and order. It may be said within my remarks that the year 1787 was a great year for rational thinking, that prerequisite for an enduring republic.

Hopefully there is a mystical strength, the greatest kind of strength, to be found by our people simply in speaking of this on a First Day in the White House—this place of great tradition, which so dramatically relates reverence and patriotism, realism and compassion. There is no other framework in which any of our contemporary problems, political, economic, or educational, can be reasonably approached. There is no need to specify the character of any of these problems when the peculiarity of each one is of lesser importance than is the matter of method common for the solving of them all. This is a difficult lesson to teach and a hard one to learn, but it seems to me we need to make very thoughtful effort to reverse the dangerous doctrine that the end justifies the means.

This is the merging point of politics and ethics where the public welfare is most at stake. In our era of internationalism it is more necessary than ever that there be compatibility between method and goal if modern statecraft is to have a reasonable chance of bringing the kind of lasting peace we all talk about. We need not list historical examples where we either lacked the simple wisdom to know the way or the courage to follow it.

But back to the philosopher. Here one usually finds himself faced with apparent contradictions of principle when moving in the company of philosophers and lawyers. It was a philosopher, by the way, who two thousand years ago first recounted a voyage to the moon. Lucian called it a true history but confessed in the preface that he wrote "of things which are not and never could have been." It was a political satirist's precautionary disclaimer, because his real subject was the stupidity of human warfare. His lunar voyagers got caught up in civil strife between the moon men and the sun men over the colonization of Venus. Now if there is something instructive in the thought, it may be the implication that after two millenniums of philosophy, men are still fighting over real estate and still dying in the name of philosophical abstractions.

But a voyage to the moon is just as feasible as a trip to Timbuktu, though perhaps somewhat more expensive. And this suggests my last consideration of the scientist. I do not mean the scientist as a man, but man as scientist. The general polity in the republic of science is democratic. Logic and corroboration are the sole tests of validity and truth. Commitments to clear communication and unreserved cooperation are essential. If scientists compete with one another, it is because they are human, not because they are scientists. But I do not wish to imply that scientists do not have emotions relative to their field. They may be said to worship truth, and their concept of elegance might well be called the beauty of simplicity.

The titanic operation now coming to its magnificent conclusion is certainly the most prodigious demonstration of the reasoned behavior of cooperative humanity in the continuing drama of civilization. Really, can such behavior be motivated only by the fact of competition and the threat of war? The great question, whose answer spells life or death for civilized man, is this: are the human mind and spirit capable of being adapted to the requirements of the machine age?

With blind precipitousness we have revolutionized our environment. It has yet to be seen whether we can effect a corresponding revolution in ourselves. If the old platitude about human nature being unchangeable is really true, then there is nothing we can do but resign ourselves to the doom that has overtaken every species whose circumstances have changed more rapidly than their powers of adaptation. The next experiment in suicide need not lack for completeness.

To face facts, however, is not to counsel pessimism. We know that human nature can be changed because history shows us that it is constantly changing. We have faith that it must and shall be changed in time to save the bright adventure of our civilization from ruin. God's image must not be allowed to go the way of the giant lizards, its predecessors.

My own faith in mankind is renewed this morning in the knowledge that countless millions of all nations are praying today, not so much that one brave astronaut may set his foot upon the moon, but that three brave astronauts may put their feet again upon the earth. And my own hope for mankind is strengthened in the knowledge that our intrepid President himself will soon go into orbit, reaching boldly for the moon of peace. God grant that he, too, may return in glory and that the countless millions of prayers that follow him shall not have been in vain.

CONGRESSMAN BUCHANAN: O thou God of the universe, whose hand has formed the earth and set the stars in their places, look with favor upon our astronauts in their great adventure. By thy power and thy mercy, crown their mission with success and bring them safely home. As Frank Borman and his team gave their witness last Christmas from outer space to all the world as to thy power and thy glory, help us as a nation in this experience to glorify thee. We thank thee for the dedication, the effort, the excellence which have been invested in the space program and for all who have had a share in transforming yesterday's impossible dream into today's reality.

Help us with equal dedication to fulfill the great American dream for all this nation's people—and to achieve for all who are riders on the earth together victory over man's ancient enemies of hunger, disease, tyranny, and war. Our Father, we pray for our President. Fulfill the gift that is in him and complete the great work that thou hast started in him. Make him a force for good among nations, toward the realization of a world of freedom for all men, of self-determination for all people, and of peace with justice in our time. For we ask it in Jesus' name. Amen.

## September 21, 1969

Prelude

Opening Remarks            THE PRESIDENT

Invocation            CONGRESSMAN GUY ADRIAN
VANDER JAGT OF MICHIGAN

Anthem       MADRIGAL SINGERS OF WALT WHITMAN
HIGH SCHOOL
*"Dona Nobis Pacem"* (Grant Us Peace) by Jon Roberts
*"A Joyful Alleluia"* by Gordon Young

Sermon            "The Spirit Matters First"
DR. CHARLES H. MALIK
Former President of the General Assembly
of the United Nations
Distinguished Professor of Philosophy
at the American University of Beirut

Doxology

Benediction        CONGRESSMAN VANDER JAGT

Postlude

The Madrigal Singers of Walt Whitman High School,
Bethesda, Maryland, have been organized since the
school opened seven years ago. Instructed by Mr.
George G. Messick, the group consists of members of
the junior and senior classes. The Madrigal Singers
perform for local school, church and community functions.

# Dr. Charles H. Malik

THE PRESIDENT: This morning we have the privilege of welcoming to this Worship Service all of the sixty country directors of the Peace Corps, who are here in Washington for a meeting, and also many of the ambassadors from the countries in which there are Peace Corps groups. We welcome you all. We are delighted that you could come.

For this particular occasion we think we have a service that is quite appropriate. We have a very young group, some of whom I imagine might be candidate prospects for the Peace Corps— one of the finest singing groups in the Washington area, the Madrigal Singers from the Walt Whitman High School.

Our speaker today, Dr. Malik, is a man who is known to everybody in this room, known because he has had such a distinguished public career. Some think of him primarily as a former Ambassador from Lebanon to the United States. Others remember him as one of the signatories of the United Nations Charter and as President of the General Assembly in 1958–59. And of course many of us here have either read his books or heard him speak with an eloquence that has seldom been matched in this quarter of the century. I have had the privilege of knowing him through his letters and also personally.

Dr. Malik was born in a very small village in a very small country, but he truly is a philosopher to the world. I present him as a personal friend and as a friend of everyone in this room— a friend of anyone who has a great desire for this world to have peace. He has worked tirelessly for human brotherhood and understanding.

Congressman Guy Vander Jagt will give the invocation.

CONGRESSMAN VANDER JAGT: O thou God of all nature and all people everywhere: Thou hast promised that where two or three are gathered together in worship of thee, there wilt thou be also. Calm our racing minds and our restless hearts that we, as we worship together, might be still and know that thou art God. From a sense of thy presence here with us this morning, may we draw a renewed dedication to the dream in fact that all men are brothers, intended by thee to live together in peace and friendship. Grant us a resurgence of love, love for one another and for thee, the source of all love and understanding and peace. Amen.

DR. MALIK: Mr. President, Your Excellencies, distinguished guests, ladies and gentlemen:

I am honored indeed to be asked to take part in this service in the East Room of the White House. The symbolism of the East Room is profound, for where would the West be without the East? Never was it more necessary, or indeed more healthy, for the West to remember that *ex oriente lux* than today. But neither can the East prosper and develop without the active assistance of all those, whether in the East or in the West, who can afford to give from their bounty. Such is the state of interdependence and interaction between East and West and North and South today that we have all become members one of another. The promotion of this organic membership in the world community is the ultimate calling of peace.

The practice which you, Mr. President, have initiated of pausing now and then for a few minutes, precisely in this center of world power, to consider the eternal verities is most praiseworthy. For time and its exigencies can only be understood in the light and peace of eternity. The momentous decisions which are constantly arrived at under this awesome roof affect not only the destiny of America but the destiny of the whole world. Before this sobering fact I humbly pray Almighty God to grant to this house and its master the necessary lucidity, detachment, and strength to fulfill what is eternally expected from America in the service of truth and justice for all men; and, further, to bestow upon him that divine sense of humor without which statecraft can hardly be practiced by mortal man, let alone endured for long.

In history it is always a matter of war and peace, but the crucial question is whether it is war for the sake of peace or peace for the sake of war. This is the deepest distinction which divides men and cultures, namely, whether peace or war is the ultimate nature of things. If peace, then man cannot rest in war, but only in peace, and war must sooner or later be transcended. If war, then man cannot rest in peace, but only in war, and peace must sooner or later be overturned.

The deepest springs from which America has drunk proclaim the rest of peace as the sabbath of the soul.

Where men and cultures differ on this point, it is humanly impossible to reconcile them. When what is in question is the question itself, then it is humanly impossible to agree. The real challenge facing the highest statesmanship today is not so much how to defend hearth and home, nor indeed how to contain and deter external material dangers, as how to make people believe in peace and rest rather than in turbulence and war, how to compose the essentially troubled soul.

I am not thinking of this or that particular situation, nor of specific measures required by the flux of events; I have in mind only the essential character of peace and war in relation to the human soul.

Peace is the perpetual struggle for the preservation and enhancement of the deepest values. Therefore it is always a matter of faith in these values, for where there are no values which man is not prepared to part with, there is no difference between peace and war: man then is like a jellyfish adjusting to and fro to every wind and wave. It is also a question of depth, for to say "deepest" is simply to admit of a scale, so that one can afford to let the deep go, but certainly not the deepest.

The deepest values to preserve and enhance, the values which constitute the very essence of peace, are five: that there is objective, reliable truth open to all men; that there is a power or disposition in man, called reason, which can grasp and assent to this truth; that man can seek and know the truth and therefore be happy only under conditions of freedom; that man is the end, and not nature, nor the machine, nor the state, nor society, nor any institution, nor any compulsive force; and that peace and not war, harmony and not discord, rest and not motion, is the ultimate nature of things.

A moment's reflection will reveal that where there is despair of truth, where reason is derided, where the original freedom of man is denied, where man himself is viewed only as a means, and where the very essence of things is conceived as perpetual change, peace is impossible. In fact, life then is not human life at all, and you would want to do something to restore to man his basic humanity.

Nor is it difficult to see that, entirely apart from any external menace, within the Western world itself philosophies have been fermenting for two hundred years or more which preach precisely these false doctrines. It is the maturing of these philosophies in the highest intellectual circles that has, more than anything else, been at the base of the tribulations which have so tragically afflicted the university in recent years. What is at stake is not so much war and peace themselves as the deepest spirit and attitude of the West in relation to war and peace.

Peace, most certainly—but the question is, how in peace, how under conditions of peace, how with the blessings of peace, how *just then not to have* your deepest values of truth, reason, freedom, man and peace themselves decay and erode. That civilization is strong and sure of itself in which these values flourish and deepen precisely under conditions of peace. And I am absolutely persuaded, knowing the United States as well as I do, that there are in America mighty reserves of spirit and mind and care which will in time stem the tide of the rampant philosophies.

Oh, come, let us reason together, let us arrive at some fixed point, let us respect one another in dignity, equality, and freedom, let us love one another because we are all men, and let us set our hearts on peace and not on contradiction and war—ah, this should be blazed today as the living motto of all those in whose hands Providence has placed the fate of nations and men.

The spirit matters first. Therefore, give me the right spirit, the spirit of truth and trust and cooperation and love, no matter how difficult and impossible the conditions, and I give you peace.

The spirit matters first. Therefore, if you are confronted with the wrong spirit, the spirit of contradiction and nihilism and hatred, then, no matter how wonderful the conditions, whether economic or social or political, peace is impossible.

A man has an over-all spirit about him—that is his character, that is his name. So has a culture, so has a philosophy, so has a total epoch. What matters first is that spirit. If it is the spirit of peace and truth, then all problems will be ironed out. If it is the spirit of radical rebellion, then peace is ephemeral indeed. Make sure first of the spirit.

The spirit is always unitary and original. How to induce the spirit of truth and trust, especially where there is rebellion against it, how to call it forth by patience and example, how to be responsive to its demands, how to plan everything in its service and for its sake; and how to exorcise the spirit of rebellion and darkness—this is the authentic task of statesmanship. One must have faith that even in the teeth of absolute negation, because the spirit matters first, the spirit of trust and love will ultimately prevail. It is always, always, therefore, a question of faith. And, I might add, only the faithful shall inherit the earth.

And yet not for one moment may one be caught napping. The

ancient dictum, "watch and pray," is of the utmost importance. For nothing is easier than to be tempted into laxity and ease when one should be absolutely on the alert. And the watching and praying should be meant, and should be unmistakably understood as being meant, only for the sake of peace.

In the end of ends one must always be humble before the will of God, for all talk about peace, like all my talk to you today, is sheer human rationalization. The peace of God is truly beyond our ken. Again and again in history the peace that supervened could never have been planned or predicted in detail in advance. And again and again the flimsy peace of man broke down because it did not correspond to the inscrutable peace of God.

Perhaps the greatest Anglo-Saxon philosopher of this century, Alfred North Whitehead, who was my honored teacher, said of peace: "Amid the passing of so much beauty, so much heroism, so much daring, Peace is then the intuition of permanence. It keeps vivid the sensitiveness to the tragedy; and it sees the tragedy as a living agent persuading the world to aim at fineness beyond the faded level of surrounding fact."

Therefore, there is no peace without the sacrifice of much beauty, much heroism, and much daring, and those who crave for peace without facing the possibility of making this sacrifice are craving the impossible. There is no peace where there is nothing permanent to justify the sacrifice. And there is no peace without sensitiveness to tragedy—the tragedy, according to the philosopher, which "persuades the world to aim at fineness beyond the faded level of surrounding fact."

Gentlemen of the Peace Corps:

I know you know that you cannot meet all the needs of the world. Nor can you impose your own scale of values. You become relevant precisely where your range of possibilities meets others' range of needs. It is there that you can throw in your two mites' worth.

I beg you to throw it in selflessly, from the bounty of your heart, with complete respect for the values of others, steering wholly clear from all politics, and accepting the price of possible misunderstanding and attack.

Let it only be said that you came in when asked for and did the best you could and asked for nothing in return.

Let it be said that a mighty nation looking after its own interests in other ways could still afford to be helpful in complete detachment from its interests. For greatness consists precisely in being so sure of yourself as to have the time and the margin to forget about yourself.

Surely this is the spirit of the Peace Corps—the joy of serving and giving in complete detachment from politics.

And if you find yourselves receiving, in terms of wisdom and experience, perhaps just as much as you are giving, do not let that disturb you, for you can never tell when or how the mustard seed will grow into a mighty tree.

We learn from each other in order to teach one another, and we receive in order one day to give. And so the unity of man across the vastness of space and time is deepened and affirmed.

And to you, gentlemen, who represent the countries which cooperate in this undertaking, permit me to say one word:

You are heirs of great cultures and traditions; hold on to your deepest values; and know with certainty that you are as much giving as receiving—giving, by permitting others to give; giving, by having given so much yourselves in the past; giving, by enabling others now to learn.

And whether rulers or ruled, whether great or humble, whether strong or feeble, whether givers or receivers, it behooves us all in conclusion to listen to the words of the great prophet Jeremiah:

"Thus saith the Lord, Let not the wise man glory in his wisdom, neither let the mighty man glory in his might, let not the rich man glory in his riches: but let him that glorieth glory in this, that he understandeth and knoweth me, that I am the Lord which exercise lovingkindness, judgment, and righteousness, in the earth: for in these things I delight, saith the Lord."

## September 28, 1969

Prelude

Opening Remarks                  THE PRESIDENT

Doxology

Prayer            THE REVEREND ALLAN R. WATSON
Senior Minister, Calvary Baptist Church
Tuscaloosa, Alabama

Hymn             *"Crown Him with Many Crowns"*

Anthem          MEMBERS OF THE ADULT CHOIR OF
CHRIST CONGREGATIONAL CHURCH,
Silver Spring, Maryland
*"O Sing Unto the Lord"* by Hans Lee Hassler

Sermon               *"One Nation Under God"*

Hymn                  *"Fairest Lord Jesus"*

Benediction

Postlude

Singing this morning are members of the sixty-voice
Adult Choir of Christ Congregational Church of Silver Spring, Maryland. The choir sang at the New York
World's Fair, Expo 67 in Montreal, toured Europe in
1966 and has performed several sacred operas on
local television. Director of the choir is Mr. Alfred
Neumann.

# The Reverend Allan R. Watson

THE PRESIDENT: We welcome all of you to the White House Worship Service this morning, and we are particularly honored to have among our guests the lady who for eight years presided with great distinction as First Lady of this house and the nation, Mrs. Dwight D. Eisenhower. We also have as our singing group, as you will note from your program, one of the finest choral organizations in the Washington area—the choir of the Christ Congregational Church in Silver Spring, Maryland.

Bringing us our message today is a man who has a double distinction. First, he is the twin brother of Congressman Albert Watson of South Carolina. Secondly, he has in the church over which he presides as senior minister, the Calvary Baptist Church of Tuscaloosa, Alabama, one of the largest Baptist congregations in the entire nation. Moreover, I find it most interesting to note that he is the unofficial chaplain of the University of Alabama football team. Many members of the team are members of his church. As a matter of fact, more than five hundred members of his congregation come from the University of Alabama.

We are very happy to have you here today, Dr. Watson—to speak not only to the older people but also with special meaning to those of the younger generation who are with us.

THE REVEREND MR. WATSON: Our Lord and our God, in a world rocked by revolution and shaken by strife, we hunger for thy peace. We long for the comfort of thy counsel. As frightened, hurt, and tired children seek refuge and rest in the strong arms of their loving father, so do we turn to thee today.

93

Waiting here in this quiet place are men and women signally honored by their fellow citizens. Please, Father, give to these executive, legislative, and judicial leaders renewed vision, strength, and purpose. We make special intercession for our President and his wife. May the devotion which makes their hearts beat as one and their simple faith in thee bring them serenity and abiding joy in the presence of overwhelming responsibility and in the midst of heartless criticism.

Give to each of us eyes to see thee, ears to hear thy still small voice, and grace and strength to respond favorably to thy call and challenge in this hour, through Jesus Christ our Lord we pray. Amen.


Reflecting upon the tremendous problems facing us today, problems such as strained and frequently ruptured international relations, racial tensions and divisions, campus disorders, and general moral decay, I for one am inclined to agree with the sentiment expressed in an old country ballad, "I've enjoyed about all of this I can stand." Or perhaps your feelings are voiced more clearly by a current hit, "Life ain't easy for a boy named Sue." Undoubtedly there are times when, burdened by the indescribable responsibilities of his office, and pressured by public opinion for omniscient and omnipotent action, our gracious host for this family Worship Service would like to sing a chorus of his own, "Life ain't easy for a boy named Richard." Come to think of it, life isn't easy for any one of us, and upon more serious reflection we would have to confess that probably it is best that it isn't so, for we are challenged thereby. As a coaching friend often says, "When the going gets tough, the tough get going." Yet, we long for a better day, a day of restoration, of stability, of peace. A day for the realization of man's personal and national ideals, a time for the securing of an abiding stability with adequate resources, and for the securing of peace. Such a day is or should be the hope of each man and the goal of our corporate life. Beloved, this glorious prospect is presented in the Scripture read a few moments ago and should capture our imagination, compel our interest, and command our attention.

One of the wonderful things about the straight talk of the Bible is that it not only presents seemingly unbelievable possibilities, it also sets forth clearly the way whereby these hopes and dreams may be realized. Simon Peter, a man cut from the same cloth as you and I, with the added advantage of having done graduate work with the Master Teacher, reveals the way in these words, "Humble yourselves therefore under the mighty hand of God."

Humility is a rare commodity indeed in our day. In an age of unparalleled scientific development, when man has moved from a stroll in the park to a walk on the moon. In a day the secularist dreamer worships himself in the laboratory cathedral. At a time when man is enamored with his tremendous achievements to the extent that he is convinced that in him dwells all good, and believes that wrong exists only in systems, institutions, and in the distribution of goods. In such a time as this, humility doesn't come easily. As long as man refuses to humble himself, he will continue to seek and to follow that which Gilbert Chesterton called, "Cures that don't cure, blessings that don't bless, and solutions that don't solve." The spirit that will open the door to a new day will come only as we look at ourselves in the light of God's perfect revelation of Himself and of His will for us in the Person of Christ. Then, and then only, will we cry out with the ancient prophet Isaiah, "Woe is me! . . . for I am a man of unclean lips, and I dwell in the midst of a people of unclean lips."

Now I do not wish to be misunderstood in what is being said or in that which I believe is set forth in this portion of God's Word. There is much which man can and should do to help usher in this longed-for new day. We must plan, we must have political machinery, there must be laws enacted, and social programs formulated. However, never let us forget that it is changed men that produce a changed society. Also, let us remember that man is not simply a creature of his environment. Rather through the power of God he may become the creator of a more favorable and desirable environment. In the light of these facts the making of a new man must be our magnificent objective, and he who has eyes to see recognizes this as a task for the divine and not for man alone.

The Greek dramatists used as a guide in their writing this principle: "Never inject a god into a play until there is no other way out." Friends, it is my conviction that we have reached the hour when we must let God step onto the stage. We have kept Him waiting in the wings all too long. It could be that we have even lost Him in the discarded props of yesterday's productions. He must get into the act. Hence, if our civilization is to survive, it is imperative that individually and as a nation, we must give the more earnest heed to this solemn admonition: "Humble yourselves therefore under the mighty hand of God."

During the administration of the late President Eisenhower, he and his wife were worshiping on Sunday in the New York Avenue Presbyterian Church of Washington. At this particular service, the minister, the Reverend George Docherty, expressed the thought that in his opinion it was only fitting and wise to add the words "under God" to the Pledge of Allegiance offered the flag of our country. The President and a large number of Congressional leaders responded to this challenge and today we proudly express our love and loyalty for "one nation under God." However, it is not sufficient merely to add words. The noble thought which they represent must be understood and acted upon. What is the significance of the expression "one nation under God"? It is not an echo of the idea embodied in our text, where the Apostle urges us to humble ourselves under the hand of the Almighty. Do not these words mean that we should recognize the vital spiritual forces that were at work in the heart and life of those who founded our nation and constituted this Republic? Does not it imply that we are to manifest a continuing dependence upon God?

These truths we readily acknowledge and yet another more

searching and revealing question must be faced. Namely: Ours shall be a nation under what kind of God? Shall it be a deity of our own creation, one who is but a reflection of our own personal desires, prejudices, and inflated egos? Shall it be a God who is but a prominent figure of the past with little understanding of and relevance to our present challenges and problems? More than a decade ago, the British theologian, J. B. Phillips, gave the answer to these questions in a simple little book: *Your God is too Small*. "These gods are too small." The cry of the needy and oppressed and the crises of our day demand a personal, living, and loving God. This God, who cares, Simon Peter met as he walked the shores of Galilee centuries ago. This very one must be and longs to be our God and guide today.

Calvary Baptist Church of Tuscaloosa, Alabama, in which I am privileged to serve as pastor, is located adjacent to the campus of the University of Alabama, home of the Crimson Tide. Upon leaving my office one Monday morning, I chanced to glance into the sanctuary of our church and noticed a student standing behind the pulpit looking first in one direction and then in another. He said nothing but continued to look this way and that. After a few moments, reluctantly the silence was broken by my question, "May I help you?" The young man answered, "I'm looking for God. I must find Him now." This wasn't the utterance of a mentally deranged man, one whom the pressures of life had driven to the point of emotional breakdown. Rather it expressed the need of a university senior, completely competent, but feeling deep within the restlessness and hunger for God of which Augustine did speak. Indescribable joy was mine as I endeavored to help him find the One whom he sought. Not a God of the mystics but the God whom I and millions of others had met in the Master. Not a God created by man's imagination or fashioned by his fancy, but the God of Abraham, Isaac, and Jacob, the God "who so loved the world that he clothed himself in human flesh and came and dwelt among us. The Promised Messiah, the

Christ, who by his death and resurrection brings life and immor-
tality to those individuals who trust him."

Under the mighty hand of such a God our nation, and we as
individuals, can experience a new birth of freedom. Without
Him, who is the Light of the world, man's brightest ideas and
most radiant schemes can only add to the blackness of the night.
Without Him, the Lily of the Valley and the Rose of Sharon,
society's garden, sown with the seed of man's most noble
thoughts, tilled by his unceasing efforts, and watered by the sweat
of his brow, can have little beauty and will ultimately end in
desolation.

A simple experience from the life of Lord Shaftsbury, a noted
British philanthropist, statesman, and social reformer, might well
summarize and bring into clear focus the teaching of this portion
of God's Word and the point of this message. Almost a century
ago, this Christian gentleman was standing at a busy London
intersection. His attention was fixed upon a little girl who obviously was desirous of crossing one of the streets. Sensing her
need of help, she looked intently at a number of men and women
but spoke not a word to them, allowing them to go on their way.
After a few minutes, Lord Shaftsbury, whose countenance reflected the concern and compassion of his heart, started to cross
the street. Quickly, the little girl looked at him and cried out,
"Mister, can I walk across the street with you?" He extended his
hand and she placed her small one in it and together they walked
confidently and safely. Upon reaching the other side of the street,
Lord Shaftsbury paused and said, "Little lady, I noticed you
looking at a number of people before asking me to help you. Why
did you ask me and not them?" "Well, sir," she answered, "you
looked so good that I felt that I could trust my life in your hands."

Ladies and gentlemen, one stands at the dangerous and de-
manding crossroads of our life today. Being a gentleman He
waits for us to invite Him into our lives. He listens for our cry for
help. Gazing upon His nail-scarred hands extended in unfathom-

able love, we too should be convinced that we can trust our lives and the future of our Republic to His care and leadership. Then, as He dwells within us and the light of His Truth permeates our plans, illumines our thoughts, and shines through our lives, the lamp of liberty and justice for all will burn more brightly beside and within the golden door.

## November 16, 1969

Prelude

Opening Remarks                    THE PRESIDENT

Doxology

Prayer            THE REVEREND HAROLD RAWLINGS
                          Assistant Pastor
           Landmark Baptist Temple, Evendale, Ohio

Hymn                      *"Rock of Ages, Cleft for Me"*

Anthem        MEMBERS OF THE ADULT CHOIR OF THE
           NEW YORK AVENUE PRESBYTERIAN CHURCH
                          Washington, D.C.
           *"Come, Come Ye Saints"* by Clayton-Prussing

Sermon              *"The World's Most Amazing Book"*

Hymn            *"All Hail the Power of Jesus' Name"*

Benediction

Postlude

The New York Avenue Presbyterian Church Choir
was founded in 1939. Singing this morning are members of the traditionally large 100-voice choir. The
choir serves not only the New York Avenue Presbyterian Church, but the community as well. Mr. Stephen H. Prussing is the director of the choir.

# The Reverend Harold Rawlings

THE PRESIDENT: Members of the Cabinet, members of Congress, members of the Diplomatic Corps, and all of our distinguished guests, welcome.

Because of the very awesome display of football yesterday in Ohio, we thought it would be appropriate today to have someone from that state to conduct our service. As a matter of fact, to be quite honest about it, in selecting our minister for today, we did not know that Ohio State was going to be all that impressive yesterday.

It happens that the man who is bringing us our message today is the youngest minister thus far to be here for our White House Worship Service. The Reverend Harold Rawlings is thirty-five years of age. He is a Baptist, and the Baptist Church is the largest of all Protestant denominations. I think it is also of interest that he is the junior member of a father-and-son team. His father, John W. Rawlings, is the pastor of the Landmark Baptist Temple of Evendale, Ohio (on the outskirts of Cincinnati), and Harold Rawlings is the associate pastor of that church. We are delighted that he can be with us this morning.

We are also fortunate to have, for the musical part of our service, the choir from the New York Avenue Presbyterian Church. It is, of course, a very famous church in terms of its background in the nation's capital, and its choir is one of the finest singing groups in the Washington area.

THE REVEREND MR. RAWLINGS: O God, our Father, it is with a deep sense
of gratitude and unworthiness that we approach thee on this Lord's Day.
We thank thee for America, our homeland, the haven of all who seek
freedom and opportunity. Make us morally worthy to protect the Republic from outward aggression and the decay of inner betrayal. Give wisdom and strength to those who have been entrusted with the
stewardship of our nation. May this service be crowned with thy presence. We ask it in the name of Jesus, our Saviour. Amen.

God has two textbooks, one the textbook of nature and the
other the textbook of revelation. The laws of God revealed in the
textbook of nature have never changed; they are what they were
since the beginning. They tell us of God's mighty power and
majesty.

In the textbook of revelation, the Bible, God has spoken ver-
bally; and this spoken word has survived every scratch of human
pen. It has withstood the assaults of skeptics and tyrants. Quentin
Reynolds once remarked, "If I were dictator, the first book I
would burn would be the Bible." Greater efforts have been made
to destroy the Bible than any other book. Yet despite the attacks
of men, through many centuries, it remains the world's most
amazing book.

It has often been reviled but it has never been refuted. It has
never bowed its head before the discoveries of science. The more
the archaeologist digs and the more the scientist discovers, the
greater the confirmation of the truth of the Bible. Dr. Nelson
Glueck, world-renowned archaeologist, expressed his faith in the
reliability of the Scriptures when he stated, "I have always gone
on the assumption that the historical statements in the Bible are
true. On that basis I have made some of my most important
finds."

The Bible has a great tradition and a magnificent heritage. W.
E. Gladstone said, "The Bible is stamped with a specialty of
origin, and an immeasurable distance separates it from all com-
petitors."

It was written over a period of sixteen hundred years by men of various backgrounds—lawgivers, kings, artisans, farmers, fishermen, and scholars. It was written in different countries under diverse social and political conditions; yet in its harmony, it is historically, doctrinally, and scientifically correct.

One peculiarity of the Bible is its claim to come from God. The writers state repeatedly that God gave them their material. Two thousand times in the Old Testament they testify that while the pen used is the pen of man, the words given are the words of God. To tell more than two thousand lies on one subject seems incredible. Either the Bible is divinely inspired, or they lied.

Jesus Christ quoted frequently from the Old Testament. He never once indicated that he doubted the Scriptures. The Apostle Paul affirmed, "All scripture is given by inspiration of God, and is profitable for doctrine, for reproof, for correction, for instruction in righteousness: that the man of God may be perfect, thoroughly furnished unto all good works." The Apostle Peter added, "Holy men of God spake as they were moved by the Holy Ghost." The Bible claims to be without a rival. It is not only a word from God, it is *the* Word of God.

The Bible is also permanent. Christ said, "Heaven and earth shall pass away, but my words shall not pass away." Helen Frazee-Bower gave poetic expression to this truth when she wrote:

> The books men write are but a fragrance blown
>   From transient blossoms crushed by human hands;
> But, high above them all, splendid and alone,
>   Staunch as a tree, there is a Book that stands
> Unmoved by storms, unchallenged by decay:
>   The winds of criticism would profane
> Its sacred pages, but the Truth, the Way,
>   The Life are in it—and they beat in vain.

Apart from its divine authority, there is more glowing eloquence, more noble sentiments, more beautiful poetry between its covers than anywhere else. Macaulay said, "If everything else in our language should perish, the English Bible alone would suffice to show the whole extent of its beauty and power."

It humbles the lofty, and exalts the lowliest. It condemns the best, yet saves the worst. It engages the study of scholars, and is not above the understanding of a little child. It shows us man raised to the position of a son of God, and the Son of God stooping to the condition of a man.

The Bible has done more to bless society, to promote brotherhood, happiness, peace, liberty, and justice in the world, than any other book, and all other books together.

Our beloved country owes more than we could ever know to the teachings of Scripture. At the Constitutional Convention at Philadelphia, representatives from thirteen colonies came together, each with his own opinion and each so dogmatic that he would not budge an inch. They had almost decided to go back to their homes and form thirteen separate nations, when Benjamin Franklin stood and said, "I have lived a long time and the longer I live the more convincing proof I see that God governs in the affairs of man, and if a sparrow cannot fall without His notice, is it probable that a nation can rise without His aid? 'Except the Lord build the house, they labor in vain that build it.' Without His concurring aid we shall proceed no better than the builders of Babel." A prayer meeting followed and out of that prayer meeting came the Constitution of the United States, whose laws and policies are based largely upon the Word of God.

Daniel Webster said, "If we abide by the principles taught in the Bible, our country will go on prospering, but if we and our posterity neglect its instructions and authority, no man can tell how sudden a catastrophe may overwhelm us and bury our glory in profound obscurity."

God speaks to man through the Scriptures. This is why it is

important to read the Bible for ourselves. Most of the time we are careful about what we eat and how often we eat, but what about food for the inner man? How easy it is to feed the body and starve the soul. Jesus said, "Man shall not live by bread alone, but by every word that proceedeth out of the mouth of God." The ancient patriarch Job had added, "I have esteemed the words of his mouth more than my necessary food."

The Word of God is the bread of life without which our spirits weaken and die, just as our bodies do if we do not eat. For this reason the Apostle Peter encouraged us to "desire the sincere milk of the word, that [we] may grow thereby." Spiritual growth is an impossibility apart from a knowledge of the Word of God.

The Bible is not only good for the soul, but oftentimes for the body as well. U. S. Army Private Roger Boe of Elbow Lake, Minnesota, is a First Infantry Division trooper in Vietnam. A few weeks ago he was on patrol near Lai Khe when North Vietnamese soldiers ambushed his unit. When the fire fight ended, Boe noticed smoke curling from his pocket. An enemy rifle bullet had gone through his wallet and lodged in his Bible, just short of a loaded ammunition clip.

It is sometimes objected that the Bible is hard to understand. It is not so hard to understand as it is hard to believe. Mark Twain made this characteristic observation: "Most people are bothered by those passages of Scripture they cannot understand; but as for me, I have always noticed that the passages of Scripture which trouble me most are those which I do understand."

Bibles are to be more than depositories of memorabilia. A little boy told his Sunday school teacher that he had learned everything that was in the Bible. He said, "Sister's boyfriend's picture is in it, so is Mom's recipe for German chocolate cake, and a lock of Grandma's hair."

The blessings of God can be claimed only where the will of God is known, trusted, and acted upon. If we wish to know what is in a will, we must read the will. If we want to know God's will on any subject, we must read His will. The word "testament," legally speaking, means a person's will. The Bible contains God's Last Will and Testament, in which He bequeaths to us the blessings of redemption. To know God's will we must study His Word.

Dwight D. Eisenhower said, "Like stored wisdom, the lessons of the Bible are useless unless they are lifted out and employed. A faithful reading of Scripture provides the courage and strength required for the living of our time."

God calls a man blessed who meditates in His law day and night. Furthermore, he is said to be "like a tree planted by the rivers of water, that bringeth forth his fruit in his season; his leaf also shall not wither; and whatsoever he doeth shall prosper." If we would only spend more time in the serious study of the Word of God, earth's questions would seem far less significant and heaven's answers far more real.

I believe the Bible to be the Word of God because it alone has the ability to satisfy the human heart. One of the great differences between man and animal is that man has the capacity to know and worship God. Every human being has an inherent cry after God. This longing for God cannot be satisfied by science and technology.

To love God and to worship Him, you must know Him in a personal relationship. For this reason the Bible was written. The Bible teaches that the only way to bridge the gap between man and God is through Jesus Christ. Jesus declared, "I am the way, the truth, and the life: no man cometh unto the Father, but by me."

The Bible is God's "love letter" to us—telling us that His love sent His only Son, Jesus, who gave his life on Calvary for our sins. "For God so loved the world, that he gave his only begotten Son, that whosoever believeth in him should not perish, but have everlasting life."

When Sir Walter Scott, the famous author, lay on his deathbed, shattered in fortune and health, he said to his son-in-law, "Bring me the Book." "What book?" asked Mr. Lockhart. "There is but one Book," was the answer.

David said, "For ever, O Lord, thy word is settled in heaven." May it also be settled in our hearts and in our nation.

In a very moving tribute to the Bible, the evangelist Billy Sunday takes a word-picture journey through the Scriptures. He describes it this way:

"I entered through the portico of Genesis and walked down through the Old Testament art gallery where the pictures of Abraham, Moses, Joseph, Isaiah, David, and Solomon hung on the walls.

"I passed into the music room of the Psalms and every reed of God's great organ responded to the tuneful harp of David.

"I entered the chamber of Ecclesiastes where the voice of the preacher was heard, and into the conservatory of Sharon and the lily of the valley's spices filled and perfumed my life.

"I entered the business office of the Proverbs, then into the observation room of the prophets where I saw telescopes of various sizes, some pointing to far-off events but all concentrated upon the bright star which was to rise above the moonlit hills of Judea for our salvation.

"I entered the audience room of the King of kings and passed into the correspondence rooms where sat Matthew, Mark, Luke, John, Paul, Peter and James penning their epistles.

"I stepped into the throne room of Revelation and caught a vision of the King sitting on his throne in all his glory, and I cried:

> 'All hail the power of Jesus' name.
> Let angels prostrate fall,
> Bring forth the royal diadem.
> And crown him Lord of all.' "

## January 11, 1970

Prelude

Opening Remarks                    THE PRESIDENT

Doxology

Prayer    THE REVEREND DR. NORMAN VINCENT PEALE
          THE MARBLE COLLEGIATE CHURCH
          NEW YORK CITY

Anthem                        THE VIENNA CHOIR BOYS
          *"Duo Seraphin"* by Ludovico da Vittoria
                    Conductor: Albert Anglberger

Sermon

Anthem                        THE VIENNA CHOIR BOYS
          *"Laudi Alla Vergine Maria"* by Giuseppe Verdi

Benediction

Postlude

# The Reverend Dr. Norman Vincent Peale

THE PRESIDENT: We are very happy to welcome all of you to the first Worship Service of 1970 in the White House, and we think it is rather appropriate that we have an old friend, Dr. Norman Vincent Peale, to bring us the message this morning. We are also delighted to have with us a very distinguished musical organization which goes back almost five hundred years, The Vienna Choir Boys. I am sure that many of you have heard them before, and this house is of course very honored to welcome them here —to bring us their message in song.

DR. PEALE: Almighty God, our heavenly Father, we invoke thy divine blessings on this service this morning. In the peace and beauty of this distinguished house, we gather for the worship of the God in whose name this nation was founded. May we feel thy Holy Presence encompassing us in this moment. We ask thy blessing upon thy servant, the President of the United States. Grant to him peace of heart, wisdom, insight, and understanding. Keep him under the shelter of thy wing. Bless this, our beloved country, that morality and idealism and religion and freedom may ever abide amongst us. And now may the peace of God, which passeth all understanding, be in our minds and in our hearts and in our land, now and forever, through Jesus Christ our Lord. Amen.

Mr. President, Mrs. Nixon, and friends: It is indeed a great honor to be here today on this the first Sunday that the White House Worship Service has been held in the year 1970—and we might also say in the new decade. I appreciate the kind words spoken by President Nixon. I have the honor to have had him for a number of years as part of my congregation. I have known him for many years, and have for him a profound admiration, as do we all, and I might add also a very deep affection for both President and Mrs. Nixon—and their family. And of course it is a privilege to hear this wonderful choir of boys from Vienna.

It seems that we have, among others, two problems today besetting people generally. One is the problem of meeting inner tension and stress and the other is the problem of standing up to the crises of human existence. In the 11th Chapter of Daniel, the 32nd verse, is a word which applies to these problems: "The people that do know their God shall be strong, and do exploits."

Take the first problem, that of tension. I suppose that you have no tension here in Washington, but we have plenty of it in New York City. I was walking down the street one day when I encountered a friend of mine, a rather high-placed business executive, and I asked him how he was. Which represented a mistake, because he proceeded to tell me. He said that he couldn't live with the tension and stress anymore—that it was really getting him, as he said. Then he waved his arms in the direction of the city and he said, "You know, the very air of this place is filled with tension."

"Well," I said, "I'll grant you that the air of this city is probably filled with pollution, but if you took the air into a laboratory and examined it, there would, I'm sure, be no trace of tension in the air."

The tension is in the minds of people who breathe the air. We are a great nation, but we are also a tense and nervous nation. I am told on reliable authority that there are consumed in this country, every night some fifteen million sleeping tablets. Now, you would think that a person would be able to lie down and go to sleep naturally. But so nervous have we become that I, who have had plenty opportunity to observe it, will tell you that you can hardly put the people to sleep with a sermon anymore. It has been years since I've seen anybody sleep in church, and that is a sad situation.

Some statistician has worked it out that we have in this country seven and one-half billion headaches every year. That works out at fifty headaches per head, per annum. Have you had your quota yet this year? Somebody has said that the Americans have a patron saint. I never thought that we did, but perhaps we do. He said the patron saint of the British is St. George. The patron saint of the Irish is St. Patrick, and who do you think he nominated as the patron saint of the Americans? Good old St. Vitus. We are a nervous, highstrung generation of people.

Of course much of our creative genius comes because of the fact that we are highly organized, but one can shake himself to pieces with tension. An athlete or a thinker will achieve the best, if he does his work with a profound inner relaxation and peace of mind.

How, then, is this achieved? Well, let me give you my answer in the form of an incident. A businessman, the sales manager of a large organization in Upstate New York, called on me to discuss with me—as a spiritual physician, as he put it—using the scientific principles of the Bible, how he could overcome tension. I discovered as I talked with him that there was a great deal of hate and resentment also in his mind—which always contributes to tension. But I found that he was extraordinarily tense. Sitting at my desk, I happened to pick up a rubber band and was rather doodling with it as he talked. Finally I said, "This is the way you are, isn't it? Like a rubber band drawn out tense and taut."

And in the vernacular, he said, "Yes, that's me all over."

"But," I said, "you'd like to be like this, wouldn't you, a limp rubber band?"

And he said again in the vernacular, "And how! Will you tell me how to do it? How to achieve peace to heal my tension?"

I think that my function as a minister is to be a spiritual physician, so I gave him a treatment. I said, "First, let yourself go limp in your chair. Let your body completely relax." And I gave him an illustration once given me by Captain Eddie Rickenbacker, who is a hard-driving man, but who does it out of peace and quiet inwardly.

Eddie said, "I slump in a chair, then I mentally conceive of myself as a huge burlap bag of potatoes. Then mentally I take scissors and cut the bag and let all the potatoes roll out. I am the limp bag that remains."

So I said to my friend, the tense businessman, "Do you think you can mentally engage in that exercise?" He said he would try. So he slumped in the chair. Now I said, "I think we'll give you a little spiritual treatment along with the physical one," and I began to quote to him certain passages out of the Scriptures. It has always been amazing to me, the medicinal, therapeutic healing quality that is to be found in these marvelous sentences by Jesus Christ, the Great Physician.

I quoted this one to him: "Come unto me, all ye that labour and are heavy laden, and I will give you rest." And this from Isaiah: "Thou wilt keep him in perfect peace, whose mind is stayed on thee." And another from Jesus: "Peace I leave with you: my peace I give unto you: not as the world giveth, give I unto you. Let not your heart be troubled, neither let it be afraid."

I felt that I saw a wistful look on the harassed face of this man. And then I proceeded to give him what I called an intellectual treatment—quoting to him statements from some of the great thinkers of the world. For example, Cicero, who said, "He who would live long and well must learn to live slowly." That is, not with depleted activity, but slowly in emotional reactions. And that marvelous passage from Carlyle which the President and I like so much: "Silence is the element in which great things fashion themselves." Then I suggested to him that he emulate the great poet, John Masefield, who said that every day he practiced the getting of tranquility.

He had told me, my business friend had, that he had made certain mistakes and, as he put it, he'd been very dumb. It so happened that at the moment I had on my desk an editorial from the late Grove Patterson, one-time editor of the *Toledo Blade.* In my opinion, that little editorial is a classic. And I read it to this man. Here's the way it goes:

"A boy, a long time ago, leaned against the railing of an old-fashioned bridge and watched the current of the river below. A log, a bit of driftwood, a chip floated past. Again the surface of the river was smooth. But always, as it had for a hundred, perhaps a thousand years, the waters slipped by under the bridge. At seasons, the current went more swiftly and again quite slowly, but always the river flowed on under the bridge. Watching the river that day the boy made a discovery. . . . He had discovered a great idea: Quite suddenly and yet quietly, he knew that everything in his life would some day pass under the bridge and be gone, like water. And the boy came to like those words, *under the bridge.* All his life thereafter the idea served him well and carried him through, although there were days and ways that were dark and not easy. Always, when he'd made a mistake that couldn't be helped or lost something that could never come again, the boy, now a man, said, 'It's water under the bridge.' And he didn't worry about mistakes so much after that. And he didn't let trouble get him down because it was water under the bridge."

By this time, we had the man's mind composed to God, to Jesus Christ. He was composed both physically and philosophically. With a slow, wistful smile, he said to me, "Okay, Doctor, I get it; it's God that will heal me, right?" I agreed. He moved toward the door, and then he did a strange, whimsical thing; he came back, saw the rubber band on my desk, and he said, "May I take this along with me?"

And I am told he actually took it to his office and framed it, that he might always see it.

But you don't need to be taught like this. By the practice of your faith, you can be quiet and have the peace of God in your heart.

The second problem is the ability to stand up under crisis. We seem to be living in a soft, defeatist kind of a time where we resent the difficulties of human existence. We resent pain, struggle, sacrifice. We resent even death. Yet all of these things are inevitable; all are natural processes. That person only can live who knows what he must face and by the help of the good God has it in him to face it. For life isn't easy, never was, isn't now. It's tough, very tough. But God and the Lord Jesus Christ are tougher than it is. And when you have them in your heart, you have what it takes to handle it.

Some few months ago, the President did me the honor of sending me to Vietnam, to visit boys in the hospitals and speak to the troops. I was glad to see that the hospitals were perhaps two-thirds empty, which indicated what the American people generally do not seem to know: that there has been tremendous progress in the pacification program there and the Vietnamization of the country. I saw vast rows of empty beds, and there's nothing more beautiful in a war zone than an empty bed.

But some of the beds *were* filled. The boys had bandages around their heads, around their arms, around their legs. There were all types of Americans. I was being followed by a couple of the military, and I asked them to remain back, so I could talk to these boys as a civilian pastor. And I sat down on the edge of their beds and talked with them. I asked them where they were from. Chatted about just generalities. I also talked to them about God. Then in each case I would ask "How are you?" I want to tell you that I talked to hundreds of boys in these hospitals, and never once did anyone say anything other than, "I feel fine." I walked out of those hospitals having difficulty holding back the tears.

But I'd always say to them, "Why do you feel fine? How come?" Again and again they would say to me something like this: "Oh, you know, the good Lord's on my side. The good Lord has His hand on me. The good God has His arm around me." That stirred my heart, too, because here were American boys brought up in the great teaching that God will see you through, and He *was* seeing them through. They had the ability to stand up to crisis.

Finally, in Vietnam, I had one of the greatest experiences of my life when I was invited to conduct a memorial service for the Seventh Marines on Hill 55, a barren eminence. Some seven hundred men were there. I arrived by helicopter, walked with the general through the massed troops to the strains of martial music. Flags were flying overhead—the American flag and the Vietnamese flag. Before me were a great valley and hills beyond bearing such names as Arizona Territory, Dodge City, Charley's Ridge, and Pipestone Canyon. I sat beside Major General Ormond R. Simpson, a man whom I liked instantly. I asked, "General, under these circumstances, when we're going to memorialize men who were killed in the recent battle of Pipestone Canyon, what shall I say to these troops?"

He said, "You're asking me! What do you think you should say to them? You talk to them about their country and talk to them about their God. They went to hear about God."

I looked down at a gun projected into the ground on which was a helmet—symbol of the dead comrades. And I talked to them about God. Suddenly—anybody who ever makes speeches will know that there are such times—there came a deep silence as if we were impinging on eternity itself. This was one of those rare moments—when all of a sudden I saw these earnest young faces looking at me with intensity, seeming to be drinking in everything that was said. I asked the Lord to help me, and I talked to them about God.

Then a big, black sergeant, a wonderful man, with one of the greatest voices I've ever heard in my life, sang, and I can hear the notes ringing out yet over those valleys and hills: "How great thou art." And I knew that we'd reached a high eminence of feeling and understanding.

Then they played taps and a volley was fired and I walked back with the general to the helicopter. I went in, strapped myself in, and then I wanted to see these men once again, for something had passed between us—love, faith. When I looked out the open side of the big helicopter, the whole regiment was at the salute, including the general.

It was the first time in my life a general ever saluted me. But I'm not the saluting kind, I'm only a civilian. So instead of saluting them, I waved to them, because to me they were just American boys, home folks from back home. And suddenly from the general on down, they broke the salute and waved back. My last vision of these men, etched there against the hills, was an aerial view of seven hundred fine honest-to-goodness men who believed in their country and in God and who had what it took to stand up to crisis.

I tell you again that the words of Daniel come ringing clear and resonant across our time: "The people that do know their God shall be strong and do exploits."

## February 1, 1970

Prelude

Opening Remarks                    THE PRESIDENT

Doxology

Prayer                THE REVEREND DR. M. L. WILSON
              Pastor, Convent Avenue Baptist Church
                                        New York City
              President, Council of Churches of the
                                        City of New York

Hymn                  *"In Christ There is No East or West"*

Verse Anthem              THE UNIVERSITY OF WISCONSIN
                                        TUDOR SINGERS
              *"Have Mercy Upon Me, O God"* by William Byrd
                    Conductor: Professor Vance George

Sermon                      *"The Arm of the Lord in 1970"*

Hymn                        *"The Church's One Foundation"*

Benediction

Postlude

The Tudor Singers represent the most accomplished
musicians from the University of Wisconsin-Madison
School of Music. The group dates back to 1933 and
sings all types of music from medieval to avant-garde.
Vance George, Professor of Choral Music at the University of Wisconsin, is the conductor.

# The Reverend Dr. M. L. Wilson

THE PRESIDENT: Our guest speaker today is a very distinguished churchman. He was born in Florida, but for the past ten years he has been in New York City. He is pastor of the Convent Avenue Baptist Church, which has one of the largest congregations in Harlem. He is now the President of the Council of Churches of the City of New York, and he is also National Chairman of the Organization of Negro Churches. He is very active in the Harlem Y.M.C.A. and is nationally known as one of our top religious leaders. We are highly honored to have with us this morning Dr. M. L. Wilson.

We are also pleased that the Tudor Singers of the University of Wisconsin, a well-known and distinguished musical group, could be here today. They are on a national tour, and luckily for us, they were able to work in a stop at the White House for this Worship Service.

DR. WILSON: God of our weary years, God of our silent tears, thou who hast brought us thus far on our way, thou who hast by thy might led us into the light, keep us forever in the path, we pray. Our gracious Father, come with us today with calm assurance. Thou art not only our Creator, but our divine earthly Father. Not until love lies dead and memory is deaf and the door of the past is closed; not until hope has lost its outlook on life and the aspirations and the desires lie in despair; and not until all that makes men noble lies in the dust—can the flame of infinite love be extinguished.

Keep before us the high standards of gentleness and forgiveness as

119

they are revealed in thy Holy Word. If we have affliction, make it mellow our hearts. Open them toward humanity. Make us more patient with the failings of other men. We ask that thou wilt bless our President, provide for him the spiritual strength so vital to carrying the responsibilities of his office. Bless his efforts as he seeks to bring peace in our time. In thy name we pray. Amen.

Today in the year of our Lord 1970, as the twentieth century moves toward its exit, we stand once more in the midst of a crisis. Across the meter of time in large red letters are the words, "TIME EXPIRED." This warning seems to be written in the heart of modern man. There is the universal feeling that history is running out, that civilization's days are numbered, that the problems of the world are insoluble, that hope has reached its frazzled end. That would be true indeed were it not for the inexhaustible resources, not of the physical universe, but of God Himself, which the Arm of the Lord does reveal.

The young people who are concerned about the draft, Vietnam, who take these questions seriously, see the issue of human life as the central one. They may have a simpler view of existence than we should like, but no matter. To them the sacredness of human life, the red blood flowing in the veins of all men, is the issue.

In the issue of student rights or the rights of youth, I don't think that many of them know the frightening effects on our culture of the disorder, violence, and intimidation. I don't think they understand that their wanton acts may provide the death blow not only to institutions, but to some fine educational leadership. And the end result may be not better but worse education.

But student unrest underlies the fact that we are dealing with a moral issue. The struggle for student rights and freedoms, and the attack on the establishment are expressions of the desire of the students to be considered as adult human beings and not merely as children, under the custodial care of a college administration functioning stuffily, or worse yet, as data processing cards.

Similarly with the race issue. The hard, even obscene things which are spoken by black racists and militants; the bitter and angry plans which are laid, these should not obscure the fact that for the blacks the issues are moral. They have been a people deprived for centuries of the right to think of themselves as having full stature before God. They may not see as clearly the terrible price of disorder; they may not see that anarchy is no respecter of color; but no matter, what they do see is that they are human beings with human rights.

Biblical faith sees the human scene as under the ultimate judgment of God. Because God is just, the valleys will be exalted and the high places made plain. Social unrest, however unwelcome and unpleasant, is a crude effort to restore the balance which injustice has destroyed. As such it must be seen as the revelation of the *arm of the Lord.*

We have been given the Gospel message with which to come to grips with the problems of our times. We have the most sweeping horizons before us. We must be the proclaimer of the Gospel, we must be in the business of breaking down the social and racial fears of men and eliminating the worthless regulation we hold in order to bolster up our pride. If we are to be heard in this time of crisis, we must cut straight across the lines, and help men to meet as men, and not as members of a particular vested interest.

The Gospel message through the years has been concerned about giving physical sight to the blind, and we have wrought miracles in this field. The Gospel message also proclaims that a greater miracle than the recovery of sight to blind eyes is the recovery of sight to blind hearts. The blind man who cannot see the sun is no more in need of an operation than the man who cannot see the light of God in the social crisis of our times, opening blind eyes and letting in light. We are called upon to be a part of the process of eliminating blindness. We must never forget that if we are to earn the affection of the masses, we must be in the places where the action is, lifting oppression and fear. The Gospel message is to set men free from injustice.

Dr. Gardner Taylor of Brooklyn, New York, put it well when he asked, "Is there a larger sin against God than to hold men responsible for the drudgery involved in building a community while denying to them the freedom of participation in that community into whose building their blood and toil have been poured? To refuse a human the liberating experience of schooling and then to hold him responsible as intellectually unfit, to sentence any soul to the bondage of living in a filthy ghetto and then to brand him as irresponsible because he is dirty, to deny a person the freedom of employment and then to hold him responsible for not being ambitious, to degrade any human soul by epithet and systematic scorn and then to demand of him dignity and to hold him responsible for breaches of personhood is a brutal violation of one's own moral apparatus and an insult to the God whose dignifying stamp is in every human soul."

As long as there is injustice in the distribution of those things which all men are entitled to, our Lord will expect us to be there fighting for the righting of those wrongs.

The Christian has the advantage over others in that he can ignore labels and go straight through smoke screens to the heart of the human situation. For under the guidance of the Holy Spirit, he follows the path of justice and righteousness, not only in his own life, but in his society. I know that when we move out into the arena where the action is, we run the risk of being called radicals and rabble-rousers, but let us remember that the prophets to whom we listen on Sunday speaking from the Word of God were similarly castigated in their day; rejected, denounced, and not infrequently killed. And let us be reminded that the Saviour we worship spoke to us from a cross because he valued truth and justice more highly than he valued public approval.

In closing his Second Inaugural Address, Lincoln said, "With malice toward none; with charity for all; with firmness in the right as God gives us to see the right, let us strive to finish the work we are in; to bind up the Nation's wounds; to care for him who shall have borne the battle, and for his widow, and his orphan; to do all which may achieve and cherish a just and lasting peace, among ourselves, and with all nations." But Abraham Lincoln could not have believed that the Civil War, however just, could achieve these ends. He must have seen, with a sort of prophetic vision, that to proclaim charity for all would mean suffering and death for some. He must have known that the man who sets out to continue God's work of reconciliation in the world is going to expose himself to murderous hatred. It was that way for him and for those who followed in his train: Dag Hammarskjöld, John Fitzgerald Kennedy, Martin Luther King, Jr., Robert Francis Kennedy.

Today in America we need a high national resolve to create upward mobility for the poor, to share the abundance of our rich land with the deprived at home and abroad. Our world is in need of patience, human understanding, faith in ourselves and our fellow man, tolerance, sympathy, the spirit of forgiveness, good-will, and above all, love. We must restore the old-fashioned "Thank you." The barriers erected out of misunderstanding, selfishness, jealousy, envy, bigotry, prejudice, and hate, these do not provide the rich soil in which unity can grow. May we get on with the business of demolishing all those things which keep us apart. May the fires in the areas where bullets are flying and men are dying be extinguished.

God says, "Then shall your light break forth like the dawn, and your healing shall spring up speedily; your righteousness shall go before you, the glory of the Lord shall be your rear guard." Then you shall call and the Lord will answer you and He shall say, "Here I am."

Almighty God, may the good order and way of life which we are seeking to establish upon the earth, bear witness of our kinship with thy divine spirit and be well-pleasing unto thee. Hear us in the name of our Blessed Lord. Amen.

*February 8, 1970*

Prelude

Opening Remarks THE PRESIDENT

Doxology

Prayer THE REVEREND DR. HENRY EDWARD
RUSSELL
Pastor, Second Presbyterian Church
Memphis, Tennessee

Hymn (Stanzas 1 and 2) *"God of Our Fathers"*

Anthems THE AMERICAN UNIVERSITY SINGERS
AMERICAN UNIVERSITY, WASHINGTON, D.C.
*"Alleluia"* by John Weaver
*"Bow My Head, O Lord"* by Sven Lekberg
Conductor: Professor Vito Mason

Sermon

Hymn (Stanzas 3 and 4) *"God of Our Fathers"*

Benediction

Postlude

The American University Singers is a chamber choir
composed of selected voices from the undergraduate
and graduate student body of The American University in Washington, D.C. Their conductor, Vito E.
Mason, is Director of University Choirs and Assistant
Professor of Music at The American University.

# The Reverend Dr. Henry Edward
# Russell

THE PRESIDENT: We are very happy to have you all here as our guests for this White House Worship Service, and I particularly want to welcome one of the fine choral groups from the Washington area, the American University Singers. They have traveled on successful trips to other parts of the United States, and we are very proud to have them here at the White House today, with Dr. Vito E. Mason, their conductor.

For our Worship Service sermon this morning, we have a very distinguished clergyman. He is the pastor, and has been for twelve years, of the Second Presbyterian Church in Memphis, Tennessee. He has spoken all over the world. He has been on several missions for the United States Air Force, speaking to our armed forces where they are stationed abroad. And he has been particularly active also in youth work for his church—and generally throughout the United States.

Dr. Henry Edward Russell comes from one of America's most distinguished families. He is the son of one of the great jurists of this country, a former Chief Justice of the Supreme Court of the State of Georgia. He has often been asked whether he is related to the Senior U. S. Senator from the State of Georgia, and I am told that he usually replies, "We are distantly related. The Senator was the fourth son and I was the thirteenth son."

We are most honored to have Dr. Russell with us for this Sunday Worship Service.

DR. RUSSELL: Almighty and Eternal God, Creator of the multiverse and universe, the giver of life, we call thee our Father and thank thee that we are thy children. We come to worship thee, and those who worship thee must worship thee in spirit and in truth—from the heart. We would come before thy throne with thanksgiving and praise, and as we meet before thee in convocation that is special, Lord, teach us how we might worship thee in daily life.

We ask thee to give thy servants who lead this great nation wisdom and power to glorify thee in all things. Help us to solve the problems that confront mankind in Vietnam, in the Middle East, and those that we have at home where races live side by side or remote. Grant that we may know thy guidance and blessing. We ask thee, our Father, to look upon us in mercy that there may be joy in our hearts. We ask thee to be with the Secretary of State as he journeys to Africa. Help our land in the matter of money, and open our eyes to know how money matters matter.

Spare us, we pray, the mistakes and pitfalls that so easily overtake us. Yea, Lord, look upon our own needs. Our sins have kept good things from us; they always do. Redeem us, we pray, and forgive us, for Christ's sake. And in his name give us victory in the battles that matter, that we may rejoice in thee. And so, God, give guidance to the words of our mouths and the meditations of our hearts that there shall be glory to thy name, peace to thy people, and power in our common life. For Christ's sake. Amen

Mr. President, I wish to thank you for the privilege of this responsibility, for the occasion of opening the Word of God and preaching to a congregation which obviously is composed of some of the most influential and powerful people on earth.

As I come from Second Presbyterian Church of Memphis, permit me now to present to you a copy of the last communication from the White House to our church, of which I know, prior to your invitation to preach here today.

It is a memorandum written by Abraham Lincoln, in his own hand, on March 4, 1864. The memorandum was written in answer to a petition sent by five members of the church requesting the return of their church, which had been occupied by Union forces. Lincoln's reply was sent to Major General S. A. Hurlbut, who endorsed it and stated that the orders of the President—which in effect restored the church to its membership—would be strictly carried out. This memorandum, or letter, was found only recently, and I thought it might be of interest.

Mr. President, you have shown sagacity in the selection of your Cabinet, and I am sure that one of them, the Postmaster General, will serve exceptionally well, as he served on my "cabinet"—as a deacon—for more than ten years at the Trinity Presbyterian Church in Montgomery, Alabama.

Perhaps I might amplify this by telling a story:

A worthy Quaker had gone out to milk his cow on a bitter winter morning. The cow had kicked over the pail once and he had patiently returned with more water, and just as he began anew his preparation for milking, the cow wrapped a long bony tail around his head and pulled the sharp wiry hairs across his cold face. He thought within himself: I may not smite this cow, nor may I curse her. As he continued with his milking the same thing happened again, and again he thought of himself: I must not smite nor curse. His exasperation had increased as the third lash of the tail stung his face and eyes, when suddenly the cow kicked the half-filled bucket of milk and landed it upon his head, drenching him. With this the Quaker looked the cow full in the face and said: "Thou knowest that I may not smite thee, thou knowest that I may not curse thee, but what thou knowest not, tomorrow I will sell thee to a Presbyterian Deacon and he will beat the H—— out of thee."

Also, Mr. President, I could not pass this service without affectionate salutation to the head of our clan, Senator Richard B. Russell, who so admirably has served our family. Doubtless, people in his public life feel they know him and his service as senator, but who can know the deep work of the heart and hand and head which he has given to our family, especially since the homegoing of our Father and Mother.

Our subject this morning is "Holy Boldness," and our Scripture is found in the Epistle to the Hebrews, the 4th Chapter. Hear a verse or two from this chapter, written just before Jerusalem was to be destroyed, to Hebrew Christians who were in danger of denying their faith and renouncing it—written from Rome, perhaps: "Seeing then that we have a great high priest, that is passed into the heavens, Jesus the Son of God, let us hold fast our profession. For we have not an high priest which cannot be touched with the feeling of our infirmities; but was in all points tempted like as we are, yet without sin. Let us therefore come boldly unto the throne of grace, that we may obtain mercy, and find grace to help in time of need."

Boldness is an indispensable ingredient for successful living. It is courage that is ready to cope with what life presents. It is the ability to face the inevitable consequences of bearing the privilege of life. It is the opportunity that God gives a man that he can get up yet again and walk in a way of service.

These people to whom the letter was originally written knew what was happening. It was a short time before Jerusalem would be destroyed and their noble temple would vanish, and all of the ritual and sacrifice that had gone into their worship would be abolished. And at the same time they were confronted with the problems of daily life and of national life, and they knew that they needed help, so they argued again and again, "let us hold fast to those things that have made us great and have made us strong."

In this modern day, we are conscious that America has had deposited to its account, by way of the forefathers, a rich spiritual capital. It has borne enormous dividends, and we have expended of these and perhaps cut into the principal, but it is our task now that we shall hold fast, knowing that diligent effort is still the indispensable ingredient of successful living. The stance of our souls must be sustained by holding fast to those concepts that

gave birth to liberty and freedom, and which grew into the significant concepts of representative government exemplified by this
republic.

We read now of a throne, a throne of grace—that we come
boldly to it with all that we have. We know the value of education.
Who doesn't? We want it. But you can take a crook and he'll steal
coal from the railroad, and you can educate a crook and he'll steal
the railroad. You will find that man's true performance must
proceed from the heart, and this appeal to the throne is that. A
throne signifies majesty, sovereignty, dominion. We don't have
thrones in civil governments as once the earth knew, but we read
in God's Word that God sitteth on the throne of His holiness. We
read that justice and judgment are the habitation of His throne.

We often read of the throne of His glory. What can the eyes
of sinful man do with that? The throne of justice? It may be white
in its purity and cold in its austere presentation. The throne of
glory can be blinding and dazzling, shimmering and flashing
before the minds and hearts and the fragile eyes of man. But the
throne of His holiness, how can sinful man grasp that? It's lofty;
it's high; it's above our attainment, towering above us in its pure
completeness. We poor creatures are too far away, blinded and
dazed by the majesty of the heavens.

There is a throne of grace which can reach the heart that must
confront all of the situations of life. Grace has a throne. God's
grace is His free, spontaneous love to those who do not merit it.
Grace embraces all of the strength and tenderness that we can
find in love, but we are enjoined to come boldly. A timid, uncertain person, quietly discouraged by danger, easily thwarted by
anxious uncertainty, learns here that he can come boldy to this
throne and find a resolute, competent spirit. Boldness is enjoined
for the salvation of your own soul. Boldness is required to keep
a nation. Here we find that God has an eternal throne that is
designated grace. We can find mercy there when we need it. We
can find help there in the time of need. To cope successfully with

the challenges of our day we can go to that throne. I suspect that we all know this and have known it for a long time.

We need motivation; we need something that will cause us to do it. What incentive moves the heart of men?

One of my favorite stories has to do with a city where the residential area and the business district were separated by a cemetery. For years men had made a practice of walking to work to avoid feeding the parking meters. One night a man called his wife and said, "Don't wait up for me, I have to work late." He worked until after midnight and then started walking the gravel path across the cemetery.

That day a man had died and his lot was in the path and the grave had been dug. In the darkness he stumbled into the grave, falling head over heels. Terrified, he jumped up and tried to climb out; he couldn't make it; he tried again, then he said, "I know my wife has gone to bed, and I could yell my head off out here and no one would hear me, and if they did hear me they would not come out." After one more try to get out, he sat down to wait till morning.

Scarcely had he sat down when he heard other footsteps on the path, and suddenly a man fell over him into the open grave. This man was terrified also, and attempted to climb out. Sitting behind him he said, "Friend, you can't get out." Startled by the voice and terrified even more, he sprang out and cried, "Who can't?"

You know, many of us make our lives content within a rut. And a rut has been described as a grave with both ends knocked out. Oh, we peep over the ridge occasionally, but if the proper motive comes, then we will understand that great word "grace." It doesn't live in a vacuum. It is right there before men. Boldness in this context rests upon knowledge, experience, and trust. It rests upon history. Those who forget from whence they came can scarcely know whither they go.

Man needs the miracle that is in this grace. Therefore, holy boldness seeks an orientation with the throne of grace which God has provided. Whatever the problems are, it's always up to a man. Whatever the opportunity is, it's always up to a man. I've used often a sermon composed of twenty letters and ten words: "IF IT IS TO BE IT IS UP TO ME." There is no way to pass beyond that truth. Every soul must come under the scepter lifted at the throne of grace—a scepter that demands truth, integrity, character, honor, and as much purity as this sordid earth can give.

We will never solve the problem of pollution, to mention one, until something is done in your soul and mine. All engineering skill and technological know-how must reside upon that element that I find in a throne of grace. Timidity and cowardice, halfheartedness, uncertain purpose, will not bring us there, but holy boldness will. Let us, therefore, come boldly unto the throne of grace that we may obtain mercy—and find grace to help us in the time of need.

Each Monday morning in our church we have a staff meeting to review the week past and to plan for the week ahead. Invariably someone will come in and say, "I have this problem with the Juniors; I have this problem with the Kindergarten; I have this problem with the Day School; I have this problem with the Choir." I've heard it so much that one day I said, "Listen, that word 'problem' is not found in the Bible once." (I was not sure I was right, but after the meeting I hurried to a concordance and found that it is not there.) But, I said, the word "opportunity" is in there a number of times. Then I asked them to think in terms of opportunities and not problems.

The very next week, someone came in and said, "Dr. Russell, I want you to help me with this 'thorny opportunity.' "

Now, if you have a problem with the throne of grace, make an opportunity out of it. Amen.

## March 15, 1970

Prelude

Opening Remarks                                    THE PRESIDENT

Doxology

Prayer                         THE REVEREND DR. BILLY GRAHAM

Hymn                          *"All Hail the Power of Jesus' Name"*

Anthem                            MEMBERS OF THE BUCKNELL
                                    UNIVERSITY CHORALE
                Bucknell University, Lewisburg, Pennsylvania
                          *"O Come, Let Us Sing Unto the Lord"*
                                by Emma Lou Diemer

Sermon                         *"God's Answer to Man's Dilemma"*

Hymn                          *"What a Friend We Have in Jesus"*

Benediction

Postlude

Singing this morning are select members of the Bucknell University Chorale from Bucknell University,
Lewisburg, Pa. The entire chorale, composed of 120
students from all departments of the University, was
founded 6 years ago. Their conductor, Allen W. Flock,
is Professor of Music at the University and also directs
the University Symphonic Band.

# The Reverend Dr. Billy Graham

THE PRESIDENT: I am happy to have with us this morning one of the most distinguished singing groups in the nation. On Tuesday and Wednesday, the Bucknell University Chorale will be singing at Constitution Hall with the National Symphony Orchestra, and 32 of the 120 members of the Chorale are here today. They are, of course, the special 32 of the 120.

We are also pleased to have as our guests members of the Cabinet, members of the Diplomatic Corps, members of Congress, and a number of ministers of some of the largest churches in the nation, who are in Washington to attend the National Baptist Convention.

And of course when we speak of the Baptist Church, that brings us to our old friend, the famous Billy Graham, who will conduct our Worship Service today.

DR. GRAHAM: Our Father and our God, we thank thee for all that this nation has stood for historically; we thank thee for the roots of our nation that go to the Old and the New Testaments of the Bible; and we pray that as we reaffirm our faith today in thee that thou wouldst bless the leadership of this nation; and we pray also that the great and overwhelming problems that beset us at this moment will find solutions. We believe that some of them will not be solved until we hear a voice from heaven to tell us this is the way—"walk ye in it." Help us to listen and help us to have the courage to do thy will.

We thank thee for the service this morning, and as we meet here we remember that across this nation in tens of thousands of churches thy

133

Word will be proclaimed; and we pray thy blessing upon every clergyman that stands to speak today and every member of those congregations.

We pray today for the peace of the world, and we pray that if it be thy
will we may have peace in our time. And we pray that thou wouldst bring
about a brotherhood among men within a spiritual context that can
bring us together and cause us to love each other. We ask it in the name
of Jesus Christ our Lord. Amen.

Mr. President, Mrs. Nixon, distinguished guests, students from
Bucknell: Thank you for that beautiful music. Last night I was at
the Grid Iron Club, and I didn't know whether it would be out
in time for this Sunday morning service. But in looking over this
audience, I'm a little bit reminded of the parrot that lived up in
the rafters of a nightclub. One Saturday night the nightclub was
bombed, and the parrot got his feathers singed and barely es-
caped with his life. He couldn't find anywhere to spend the night
except in the rafters of the Episcopal Church. Finally he got to
sleep, but the next morning the doors of the church opened and
people began to come in, and the parrot looked very curiously
at the whole situation. He saw the choir arrive, and he said to
himself, "My, the chorus girls are different this morning." The
minister came in and sat down in his place, and he said, "My, the
bartender is even different." Then he looked out over the audience and said, "Well, the same old crowd."

I want to take as my text this morning probably the most
familiar passage of Scripture in all the Bible. It was written by the
King of Israel many centuries ago. All the problems that beset his
nation, all the difficulties that beset him personally, all the pressures that he felt—these were all so great that he went out on the
hillside that he remembered when he was a boy, shepherd boy.
And David sat under the stars and wrote this famous psalm. Here
is what he said: "The Lord is my shepherd; I shall not want. He
maketh me to lie down in green pastures: he leadeth me beside

the still waters. He restoreth my soul: he leadeth me in the paths of righteousness for his name's sake. Yea, though I walk through the valley of the shadow of death, I will fear no evil: for thou art with me; thy rod and thy staff they comfort me. Thou preparest a table before me in the presence of mine enemies: thou anointest my head with oil; my cup runneth over. Surely goodness and mercy shall follow me all the days of my life: and I will dwell in the house of the Lord for ever."

In this brief passage that David penned, he touched on the three basic problems that confront you and me and our world today.

He faced the problem of human iniquity that causes lust and greed and jealousy and envy; that leads to racial tension; that leads to war among nations—which has plagued the human race from the very beginning of time. He touched on that when he said, "He restoreth my soul."

Then he touched on the suffering of the human race. Ever since Adam and Eve looked on the lifeless body of their son, killed by their other son, man has been killing and pillaging and raping all down through the centuries. Every generation seemingly has to fight it out. In spite of all our technological advances, man still suffers. He can have affluence, but there are psychological sufferings. Even the most affluent suffer, and the pain is even greater sometimes than for those who are in poverty. David said in effect, "I shall not want, no matter what my circumstances. I have found fulfillment."

And the third problem we all face: "I walk through the valley of the shadow of death . . . thou art with me." German theologians are writing today about ultimate situations in life that cannot be changed, and death is certainly one of them. We are going to die. The Bible says it is appointed unto man once to die. David said he found the resource to help him face death.

First, "He restoreth my soul." When they were having the riots in Berlin, someone asked a student leader why they were rioting, and the student said, "Germany has lost her soul, and we are going to restore the soul of Germany." We hear a great deal today about soul and soul music. I asked a Negro friend of mine what soul meant. We were standing on a street corner in Harlem. He said soul means everything worth while that's in a man. And, you know, nations have souls.

America's soul: patriotism, morality, respect for law, faith, social justice, brotherhood among people of diverse backgrounds. This is the very soul of America but we are in danger of losing our soul, and the boys in the military may soon ask if it is worth dying for. Unless our soul is restored, the best men in America will begin to ask if it is worth going into politics for. *Unless our soul is renewed and restored.* Jesus asked the question long ago: What shall it profit a man or a nation if they gain the whole world and lose the soul.

And in a personal sense, too, we all have souls. You have a soul and I have a soul. You have a body, but living down inside your body is a spirit, a soul that is eternal, and whether you like it or not, you are going to live forever somewhere.

The Bible teaches that our souls have been separated from God. In the very beginning of the human race, man rebelled against his maker. Our souls are separated and as long as that remains true we cannot find fulfillment and satisfaction. You can become a wealthy man, a powerful man, but you will never find the fulfillment until your soul has been restored.

And that's what Good Friday is all about—that we are going to be celebrating next week. When Jesus Christ died on that cross something supernatural happened. The Bible tells us that God took all of our sins and laid them on Christ. In that moment, God can say to you, "I forgive you of every sin and every rebellion in your heart. I forgive you because Christ took it on that cross. That's what we celebrate Good Friday for. That's why every Roman Catholic and every Protestant makes a great deal of Good Friday—because we believe that on the cross Christ died to restore our souls. And I hope that every one of you, individually, will come to the foot of that cross and say, "O God, I have failed, I have sinned, I want forgiveness." He loves you and He *will* forgive you and restore your soul.

Then the second thing David said: "I shall not want." Now, we as a nation are facing many social problems today—poverty, racial tension, war, crime, the ecological problems that we are all talking about. But we also have personal problems that would come under this statement, "I shall not want"—boredom, guilt, loneliness, a marriage that's gone wrong; bad health, dreams unfulfilled, a friend that betrayed you, the pressure of life that seems too great to bear at times, one of your children that disappointed you. Job said man is born unto trouble. We all have problems. We all have pressures.

I was standing on a great university campus the other day with the dean of the university and I asked him, "What is the greatest problem that the students at this university face?" He thought a moment and he said, "Emptiness." *Emptiness!* Looking for something but not finding it! You know, there is a consciousness of an ultimate emptiness in life that is reflected in modern art and literature and philosophy and life as a whole.

A girl came from a fine college to her parents, and she was crying bitterly. She said she was dropping out of school. She cired for a whole day, and in the evening, finally, the father was able to penetrate her gloom, and she looked up in desperation and she said, "Daddy, I've had it all, but I want something and I don't know what it is." Most of us are that way. We get to certain goals in our lives, but there is something else we haven't found. What is it? God. You were made for God, and without God you won't find that fulfillment.

The more affluent a society is, the more pronounced is the sense of ultimate emptiness on the part of its members; and to escape this sense of emptiness and alienation, thousands are turning to drugs, thousands are even turning to suicide.

David had found the strength as the King of Israel, and Israel was at the height of her glory then. David said, "I found the strength in my relationship to God, and I can say, 'I shall not want.' " Hundreds of years later, in a cold, rat-infested prison in Rome, the Apostle Paul said, "I have learned in whatever state I find myself to be content." He had found a contentment.

I meet people all over America—I meet them in the homes of the rich and I meet them in the homes of the poor—who say, "I've found this same contentment. I can say with David, whatever my circumstance, I shall not want."

I believe, however, that the spiritual famine throughout our nation is of greater seriousness and more far-reaching consequence than any specter of war or even crime that faces us. Spiritual leanness haunts millions. The starvation of the human mind and soul has reached alarming proportions, in my judgment. Is there something we can turn to? I say there is. God! And we *can* say, "I shall not want." The great problem, as the President expressed it in his Inaugural Address, is a crisis of the spirit.

And then the third problem that David said he had found an answer to was death. "Yea, though I walk through the valley of the shadow of death . . . thou art with me." Death began when man rebelled against God. God never meant that we would ever die. We were created to live forever, created in a perfect environment. But when man rebelled, as a part of His judgment God said, "Thou shall die. You are going to suffer, you are going to die. Every generation will die." And so we are all under that same sentence. It is appointed unto man once to die.

And, you know, it's an interesting thing to me that death has become the forbidden subject of our generation. Just as we tried to suppress the idea of sex in Victorian times, we are trying to suppress the subject of death in our own times. We try to run away from death, and we make a cult of automatic progress. Many people think that they are facing death when actually they are sidestepping it with the old "eat, drink, and be merry, for tomorrow you die" attitude: middle-aged men and women who want to love everybody, go everyplace, do everything, hear everything, or even get a new mate before the end comes. It's like the slogan, "If I have only one life to live, let me live it with a blonde."

Even the psychiatrists seem reluctant to talk or write about death, and in many textbooks on psychology there is not a single paragraph on the subject of death. Yet that's the greatest problem you're ever going to face. That's the greatest battle you'll ever fight. Nobody can fight it with you, nobody can go there with you. You've got to face it, and yet we don't prepare people for it. We don't prepare ourselves. We try to get it out of our minds. A great English psychoanalyst believed that the fear of death is at the root of all human anxiety. Yet the Bible states that there is an answer to the problem of death.

Even young people are singing songs about death. What are they singing? Listen to those lyrics if you can get the words through the rock beat. I buy a little paper called *Song Hits* once in awhile just to see what the latest lyrics are, and you would be amazed at how many of them have to do with death. Young people thinking about death, singing about death, but few are giving them answers.

Two weeks from today we are going to celebrate Easter. I believe that on that first Easter death was conquered. I believe that Jesus Christ literally, physically, arose from the dead and is alive now.

One time during his final years in office, Chancellor Adenauer invited me to come and see him. I had never met him. I did not ask for the appointment. I did not know he knew I existed, but I went to see him. We had a cup of coffee, and he suddenly turned to me and he said, "Young man, do you know why I invited you here?" I said, "No, sir." He said, "I want to ask you this question: Do you believe that Jesus Christ is alive now? Do you believe he arose from the dead?" I said, "Yes, sir." He said, "So do I," and he added, "When I leave office, I am going to spend the rest of my life proving that He is alive, because I believe it can be proven."

Those of us who had the privilege of going to visit General Eisenhower in his last days at Walter Reed Hospital will never forget the courage with which he faced the greatest battle of his life. And the reason he had that courage, in my judgment, was that he had an inner resource and an inner faith that helped him. "Yea, though I walk through the valley of the shadow of death, I will fear no evil: for thou art with me; thy rod and thy staff they comfort me." Thus to man's eternal dilemma—iniquity, suffering, death—David had found an answer.

I don't think everything in America is hopeless, as some people seem to believe. Our moral and spiritual sickness can be cured. If we could have a revival of genuine faith in God and a return to moral principles, if we could say individually, "The Lord is my Shepherd," and say collectively, "The Lord is our Shepherd," I believe the American people could be brought together. I don't think there is any problem that divides us that couldn't be vanquished in the heat of a great spiritual awakening, renewal, and revival. It could begin in your heart and mine today. The Lord could become your Shepherd.

# April 5, 1970

Prelude

Opening Remarks ............................ THE PRESIDENT

Doxology

Prayer ............. HIS EMINENCE JOHN CARDINAL KROL
Archbishop of Philadelphia

Hymn ........................ *"A Mighty Fortress Is Our God"*

Anthem ............... MEMBERS OF THE SANCTUARY CHOIR OF
ST. PAUL'S UNITED METHODIST CHURCH
Kensington, Maryland
*"Springs in the Desert"* by Arthur Jennings

Sermon ............... *"With Firm Reliance on the Protection
of Divine Providence"*

Hymn ........................ *"Joyful, Joyful, We Adore Thee"*

Benediction

Postlude

Singing this morning are members of the Sanctuary
Choir from St. Paul's United Methodist Church in
Kensington, Maryland. Captain Dale Harpham, Choir
Director, serves professionally as Assistant Director
of the United States Marine Corps Band.

# His Eminence John Cardinal Krol

THE PRESIDENT: I am very happy to welcome all of our very special guests to this Worship Service in the White House—and particularly Chief Justice Earl Warren and Mrs. Warren. And of course this house is especially honored to have with us again President and Mrs. Johnson. And, Mr. President, I want you to know that in these great Sunday services we have been thinking of you, and we are very pleased to see you return once more. You will be in my thoughts and prayers.

We have for our music today a very fine choral group from St. Paul's United Methodist Church of Kensington, Maryland. It is of particular interest, I think, that the director of this choir is Captain Dale Harpham. He has been a Marine Corps captain for twenty years, and by Act of Congress, which I have just signed, he will be a major after this service.

Shortly after I had met today's very distinguished guest speaker, I was talking with Cardinal Cooke in New York, and I told him how impressed I was with the conversation I had had with Cardinal Krol. I added that he was very logical—that he talked just like a lawyer. And Cardinal Cooke smiled and said, "Well, he should." He then explained that Cardinal Krol is probably the outstanding expert on canon law in his church. Consequently, I present him to you today not only as one of the nation's and world's great religious leaders but also as one who is expert in many areas.

This house is highly honored to have, conducting our Worship

143

Service this morning, His Eminence John Cardinal Krol, the Archbishop of Philadelphia.

CARDINAL KROL: Lord God, Creator and Supreme Governor of the Universe, we your children have gathered in your name to fulfill our first and foremost duty—that of giving praise and glory to you. Lord, you have said where two or three are gathered for my sake, there I am in the midst of them. We acknowledge your presence. Abide with us, and spare us, and sanctify us. Help us to detach our minds and hearts from the many preoccupations of our daily lives. Help us to avoid distractions in our effort to reflect on your truths. May our lips in prayer bless your name. Cleanse our hearts from all vain thoughts so that we can focus all attention upon you, and lighten our minds, strengthen our wills, and kindle our affections so that we may worthily and devoutly participate in this religious service. We acknowledge our total dependence upon you as the source, the continued support, and the ultimate goal of life.

With sincere repentance we humbly acknowledge and beg forgiveness of all our faults and iniquities. Be merciful to us, O Lord. Grant that this religious service may increase our knowledge of you, and love for you, that it may help us to know and to conform to your will, that it may help us to carry with serenity the burdens and crosses of life—and to accept adversity as well as prosperity with supreme confidence that you will convert all crosses into crucifixes of salvation for our best spiritual interests. Amen.

"Unless the Lord build a house, they labor in vain who build it." My dear brothers and sisters in the Lord:

Almost two hundred years ago, the foundations of this nation were laid on a self-evident principle that all men equally are creatures of God and are endowed by God with certain inalienable rights which governments must ensure. Our founding fathers knew that a political system built without reference to God would be at best a house built on sand. Thus at the beginning of the Declaration of Independence, they appealed to the laws of Nature and Nature's God. At the conclusion, they expressed a firm reliance in the protection of divine providence.

For them, Nature was an open book of divine revelation, with very obvious and compelling evidence of God's existence, indeed, of His presence in the world. For them, man was endowed by God, not by law or a government, with inalienable rights which government must respect and protect. Rights inalienable because man is made in the image of God as a reflection of the divine Creator. He is not a creation of the state. For them, divine providence was nothing less than the continuing and loving presence of God in the world He created and for which He unceasingly cares. The timeless conviction about God to which this nation's founders subscribed can probably be best summarized in the words of St. Paul to the Romans. He wrote that ever since God created the world, His invisible qualities—both His eternal power and His divine nature—have been clearly seen. Men can perceive them in the things that God has made.

It is indeed providential that the founders of this nation had such a firm understanding and grasp of fundamental truths. From the very depth of their convictions came a passionate concern for a recognition of man's dignity and for the protection of his freedom. Each man is sacred. Each man's dignity is inviolable. Each man's soul is immortal. The state exists for man, not man for the state.

Law is not an arbitrary imposition of irksome obligations; it is a reasonable norm for a balanced exercise of ordered freedom. Law is a protection against every excess or abuse of freedom which tends to degenerate into license. Law is a criterion for distinguishing between protest and revolt, between dissent and anarchy, between demonstration and destruction, between violence and nonviolence. Even the law enacted by human authority was, in the mind of the founders of this nation, to be judged by the conformity to the transcendent principles of the laws of Nature and of Nature's God. This fact is most evident in the Bill of Rights. It is implicit in the very nature of the Constitution—a fundamental statement of constitutive principles—which cannot be abrogated and to which all subsequent legislation must conform.

The concern for the dignity of the human person, for his individual liberty, for personal integrity—this concern endures today. The dedication to the principles of equality and liberty enunciated in the Declaration of Independence is not a dead letter, it is a continuing, living reality. The dedication is reflected in the increasing concern for the rights of the disadvantaged. In this century there has been significant progress in improving the lot of so many members of our society: the orphans, the mentally retarded, the emotionally ill, the aged and the sick. Such institutions as the National Labor Relations Board, the multiple programs of the Department of Health, Education and Welfare, the Office of Economic Opportunity, Social Security, Medicare, Medicaid, all of these are some of the more important milestones in our continued dedication to the principles of the Declaration of Independence. They reflect our efforts to respect human dignity.

Though the results are gratifying, and do indeed bear eloquent witness to our concern and our efforts, the task, as each of us will readily admit, is not complete. In our generation of instant remedies, there is a tendency to demand instant completion and perfection of all our unfinished business, of all our unfinished work, to have everything done *now*. Though we must be constant in our interest and efforts, only a totalitarian form of government claims to produce instant cures for social ills. This was once explained in a communist classroom by a little lad when he was asked what was the genius of the communist system. He said the genius of the communist system is its ability to solve problems which other nations do not have.

The processes of our form of government are not those of arbitrary dictatorship, nor would we exchange our processes, which are deliberate, for those of a totalitarian state.

Is there not in our system an increasing sensitivity to the need of financial security as a guarantee of personal dignity? Is there not a greater awareness that enforced separation implies and creates tragic inequalities? Is there not an ever more refined appreciation of the rights of conscience? Is there not an evident idealism among those who generously and willingly dedicate themselves and their lives to the service of the hungry, the lonely, the sick, and the abandoned? Do not many of the activities of dedicated men and women reflect the presence of the virtues which our Lord called blessed, and yet do we not experience a gnawing disquiet, a vague uneasiness?

Some of our actions seem to be based at times on hasty improvisations rather than on traditional foundations. When we are inclined to assume that money is a universal antidote, we confess that our diagnosis of the illnesses which afflict our society is not complete and totally accurate. A material remedy is not a cure for spiritual poverty. The hunger of our souls cannot be satisfied with the indigestible food of our affluence. Man does not live by bread alone. The first virtue which our Lord called blessed was the poverty of spirit. Blessed are the poor in spirit means blessed are they who recognize that their sufficiency is from God, that without God they are nothing, and that apart from God, their efforts build structures on sand.

As we seek more and more to cure the ills of society with merely material remedies, we run the danger of adopting—certainly not by design but by default—the erroneous principles of the totalitarian societies whose actions we abhor. Such societies are dedicated to an atheistic, materialistic prospective of life in which the state is supreme and human life is governed, not by the changeless laws of Nature and Nature's God, but by the dictates of an elite of political and social engineers for the benefit, not of the people, but of the state. Is there no dimension to man but the material? If there is not worth in man except in what he is able to produce, if human rights are alienable and rescindable by the state, then man would appear, not as a creature and a reflection of God, but as a creature of the state, living by tolerance of the state and living for the benefit of the state.

If God is not acknowledged as the foundation of man's dignity, then man has no authentic claim to true dignity, to his immortal destiny, to inviolable integrity. If God is not acknowledged as the foundation of human society, then society cannot claim true authority, and there can be no ordered liberty, and no viable polity.

Government without God can come into existence. It can survive for a time. It can and has caused mischief and misery. Government without God can even make great progress toward world domination, but such a government contains a fatal error. It contains within itself a suicidal ingredient. To survive, such a government must increasingly invoke physical force and violence, and apply it to those it would govern. Such a force can paralyze, it can stun, it can kill the body, but it cannot kill the spiritual forces or man's natural desire of expressing the liberty and the freedom that God gave him.

Government cannot exist without God, or be forced to attempt to provide a substitute—a counterfeit. It may attempt to provide a substitute by deifying the state—and citizens will soon discover that the idol has feet of clay; or it will deify the majority—and the minority will become mercilessly crushed and ungovernable; or it will deify the ruling elite who will insist on being served—rather than serving—and absolute power will result in absolute corruption.

When a nation loses sight of its spiritual values; when it ceases to strengthen its spiritual foundations; when it permits a depletion of its spiritual capital; when it makes little effort to replenish these reserves and to have them permeate the lives of the people, then not by design but by default it opens the door to the influence of materialism which denies man's dignity and his destiny. The first impact as evidenced by history is totalitarianism—a substitution of naked power for the loving authority of God. The authority of God guides conduct, and guarantees freedom; the unfettered power of a materialistic state forces compliance, and suppresses liberty.

Historians will judge our generation not so much by our Gross National Product, nor by the Cost of Living Index, nor by the size of our arsenals, as by our dedication and contribution toward the general welfare—domestic tranquility—and our efforts to secure the blessisngs of liberty through justice and peace in the nation and in the world. Though our efforts are relentless, and at times reach heroic proportions and progress is notable and gratifying, we must humbly admit that in some areas we are losing ground. We cannot, for example, ignore the dramatic increase in violence and in violent crimes. In the past nine years, there was a 13 percent increase in population, but a 131 percent increase in violent crimes. Many studies have been made, many explanations given, many solutions offered. All agree that crime and violence are serious problems of our generation.

Again in our age of "instant cures" there are those who look for some form of a scientific breakthrough by specialists—some crash program to solve the crime problem. It is vain to look for such a "miracle" solution. The approach must indeed by a multiple one. It must direct our anticrime energy with adequate balance to the task of prevention as well as to the task of combating crime.

The task of prevention, to be effective, must include a concerted effort to teach the difference between right and wrong. We must impress the reality of the personal responsiblity of every creature to his creator. We must try to help all to know the fundamental principles of religion and morality, those on which our nation was founded—and to translate them into a code of personal and community action, and to permeate the life of individuals and society with these religious and moral principles.

To accomplish this religious education, church membership and church attendance are useful and necessary, but not sufficient. Faith itself is necessary but not sufficient. Faith without works is dead. Even faith which moves mountains avails little without charity. Religion and morality must be allowed to permeate and penetrate the lives of our people and our society. Men must be taught to respect moral order, to be obedient to authority, to love freedom, to come to decisions in the light of truth, to govern their activities with a sense of responsibility; and, both individually and in cooperative effort with others, to strive after what is true and right.

Men must learn to appreciate the fact that law is a strong support and protection of individual freedom. In brief, our antipoverty efforts must be directed to spiritual as well as to material poverty. Our President recognized the pressing reality of this spiritual poverty last January in his State of the Union Message. By his leave, I quote his words: "Even more than the programs I have described today, what this nation needs is an example from its elected leaders in providing the spiritual and moral leadership which no program for material progress can satisfy." The President was re-echoing the admonition of the Psalmist: "Unless the Lord build a house, they labor in vain who build it." Equivalently, the President said, God, the supreme factor in the universe, must also be the supreme factor in our individual and national life.

It is perhaps providentially significant that the very symbol of American materialism should carry a reminder of the foundation which this nation's architects recognized and on which they built and we must build. Do not the currency and coins in our pockets proclaim the striking truth *in God we trust*?

Grant us, we beseech thee O Lord God, an understanding that knows thee, diligence in seeking thee, wisdom in finding thee, a way of life that is pleasing to thee, perserverance that faithfully waits for thee, and confidence that we shall be forever united with thee. Bless us, O Lord, so that we may leave this worship service with joy, inspiration, encouragement, and determination to please thee in all things and to attain everlasting reward for deeds well done, and for a life well lived. Amen.

## April 26, 1970

Prelude

Opening Remarks                    THE PRESIDENT

Doxology

Prayer              THE REVEREND JOHN A. HUFFMAN, JR.
              Pastor, Key Biscayne Presbyterian Church
                              Key Biscayne, Florida

Anthem            MEMBERS OF THE LAURENTIAN SINGERS
              St. Lawrence University, Canton, New York
              *"O Magnum Mysterium"* by Luis De Victoria

Hymn                        *"Onward, Christian Soldiers"*

Sermon                          *"Dare to be a Daniel!"*

Anthem                        THE LAURENTIAN SINGERS
              *"Hallelujah"* by William David Brown

Benediction

Postlude

The Laurentian Singers, directed by Dr. G. Errol Gay, are now in their 25th year. They have given three performances before Canada's Parliament, the first choral group to ever appear in the halls of the Canadian House of Parliament, and have toured extensively throughout the eastern United States and parts of Canada. Thirty members of this 50-voice *a cappela* choir are singing this morning.

# The Reverend John A. Huffman, Jr.

THE PRESIDENT: I am very happy to welcome all of you to the White House Worship Service today. The service this morning is one that was scheduled for last Sunday but was postponed due to the fact that we had to be in Hawaii to greet the astronauts of Apollo 13. Consequently, I particularly want to express my appreciation to the Reverend Mr. Huffman and the Laurentian Singers for returning to us today.

Many of our guests traveled a long way to be here for the service last Sunday, and some of you have come back today. We are most appreciative, but of course Washington at this time of year is worth visiting twice.

The man who brings us the message today is one many of us know. He is one of the youngest ministers ever to appear in this room. He has, however, traveled broadly throughout the world. Moreover, he has been particularly effective in bringing messages to young people. His early record impresses me in a number of respects. He attended Wheaton College, the Woodrow Wilson School of Princeton, and Princeton Theological Seminary. His scholarship was outstanding; yet he won nine varsity letters and was also active in student government.

I think it is very appropriate that we also have with us this morning the Laurentian Singers from St. Lawrence University at Canton, New York. They have been one of the outstanding singing groups in the nation for the past twenty-five years. They have given three performances before Canada's Parliament and were

153

the first choral group ever to appear before that body. They have toured extensively throughout the eastern United States and parts of Canada.

We warmly welcome both the Laurentian Singers and the Reverend John A. Huffman, Jr., pastor of the Key Biscayne Presbyterian Church of Key Biscayne, Florida.

THE REVEREND MR. HUFFMAN: Gracious Father, we thank thee for life, for liberty, and for the opportunity to pursue happiness. Forgive us for our tendency toward distortion, which causes us to mistake our own selfish interests for the true life, the true liberty, and the true happiness which are to be found through faith in Jesus Christ.

We thank thee for this hour of worship in which we turn our minds from earthly matters to matters of the Eternal, therein receiving a recharging of our spiritual batteries to pick up once again our day-in, day-out routine duties. Sanctify this room to its special use, that matters of partisan and social interest may be temporarily set aside, making this a sanctuary of authentic worship. Make these White House worship times a special spirtual re-creation for our President and his friends.

Our Father, we remember to thank thee for answered prayer on behalf of our astronauts, that thou hast brought them back safely, saving them and the world from what could have been a tragedy of horrendous proportion. And we thank thee for the exciting fact that, even in a day of calculated skepticism, the natural reflex of men and women all around the world was to pray to thee for help, thou who art a powerful, personal God.

Now as life moves on, may we not become callous to the crisis nature of modern existence. May we walk amid the confusion and relativity of fast-moving events with a sense of thy stability, thy authority, thy love, and thy help. Give to our President and all public officials that humble steadfastness of purpose that will put commitment to Jesus Christ and the welfare of our fellow man above every other consideration. Hear our prayer, a prayer which we pray with thanksgiving in the name of our Saviour and Lord, Jesus Christ. Amen.

Some of you, when you were in Sunday school, probably sang a little song that many youngsters are singing this morning titled "Dare to be a Daniel." It goes: "Dare to be a Daniel;/Dare to stand alone;/Dare to have a purpose true;/And dare to make it known." It's a story about a young man, a Hebrew lad who lived about six hundred years before Jesus. He lived in the area of Jerusalem. As a teenager his country was invaded by a Babylonian king named Nebuchadnezzar. Nebuchadnezzar put Jerusalem under siege and for a period of months held this capital city of Judea. Then word came from Babylonia that he needed to get back. Matters of a domestic concern were pressing. So he lifted the siege, exacted tribute from the Jews, and took with him as captives a number of the finest young Hebrew lads. One of these was Daniel, sort of an early type of Wernher von Braun—or some of the missile experts of Germany. Not that we took them captive, but after World War II, Russia and the United States wooed some of the finest scientific brains of Germany.

This young man, Daniel, and some of his associates—young men who were strong of physical stature, men who were strong in mind, and even some who had knowledge of science—these men were taken to Babylonia. Nebuchadnezzar had the idea that if for three years he trained them, they could emerge as statesmen of the highest order. He did one thing, though. He changed their names, trying to strip from them the religious and national acculturation of the Jewish people, endeavoring to make them over into Babylonians.

Daniel aspired to statesmanship. He had ambition. He had high goals. But one thing he would not do. He would not compromise the integrity of his convictions, his personal faith in the Lord God of Abraham, Isaac, and Jacob. The Bible says very simply in a phrase that is etched through all human history, "But Daniel purposed in his heart that he would not defile himself."

Daniel, I believe, presents a picture for each of us today, of what it is to be a man of strength and courage. For Daniel not only maintained these convictions in his early life, but a new day came. Babylonia fell. The Medes and the Persians rose to power. And Daniel, with this kind of conviction, emerged and stayed in power for years as a statesman of the highest order. Here was a man who in his youth said he would not defile himself, and a man who held to that kind of principle and character all through his life, establishing the confidence of the temporal powers that came and went.

God wants you to be a Daniel. God wants you to have a purpose true for your life. What is your purpose for living? Have you stopped and thought about it recently? What is the motivating principle that's behind your life? Is it social prestige? It's tempting. It is political power? It's tempting. Let's be frank. Is it sex? For many people in our society today, men in high positions or low positions, there's that preoccupation with the secretary or someone else—an obsession that drains creative energies and becomes the dominant purpose of life.

What is your purpose in life? What is that principle that moves you on? Granted, for those of us who have an interest in politics, political power is a fascinating study. And the Bible isn't against any of these things. God isn't against any of these things that we've mentioned here. What He does do is call you, if you are a Christian, to a kind of purpose that is the highest priority of your life. Then all these other things—and you can mention many more—fit into place underneath the highest purpose of serving Jesus Christ and your fellow men. This is the greatest purpose your life can have. So when we get into the area of political power and read Plato's *Republic* on down to Machiavelli's *The Prince* and on to the modern-day Neustadt's *Presidential Power,* we extract the principles and use them—but to the great end of the service of God and the service of our fellow men.

I personally am convinced, along with a number of others, that our nation is rapidly developing a spiritual vacuum. I'm convinced that this vacuum, to a large degree represented by our youth, really comes right back to haunt us as far as its cause is concerned. Dr. Robert Gould of Bellevue Hospital in New York City says there's a spiritual emptiness in the home, a loneliness, a lack of communication and plain unhappiness which is covered up by material possessions and frantic running around. He states there's ". . . not a home I know of where parents do not either drink or smoke cigarettes, have barbiturates to go to sleep, tranquilizers to get through the day—not aspirin, but mood-changing drugs." And we wonder why our kids turn on.

Dr. James Masterson of Cornell Medical Center states that parental permissiveness, inconsistency, punitive discipline, affluence, tension, and lack of love all guarantee trouble. You know, we get worried about our young people. We're concerned about what's going to happen to the youth of America. We want something to happen to the kids. But how many of us are willing to let this thing happen to us. have our lives changed by the power of Jesus Christ, so that we have purpose and direction for living?

A mother came to me a few weeks ago and she said, "Mr. Huffman, I'm desperately concerned about my teenaged son. He's thirteen. He's all caught up in problems. The gang he's running around with is not the right gang." She added, "I don't know what to do. I need your help. I hear you have a youth minister who's coming here, and I'm going to ask you to straighten out my son."

"Well," I said, "let's talk about you for a moment. Have you given your life to Jesus Christ? Do you have a purpose?"

She said, "Don't you talk about that to me. I'm here to talk about my son, and now you're going to bother me. You just want money for the church. That's all you want."

I said, "Really, that's not what I'm interested in. If your son is to have direction for life, he needs to see that kind of direction in your life."

She stalked out of my office and has never been back.

This is what the kids see today. They see a double standard.

They see phoniness on the part of some of us, in that we want *them* to have a motivation and a purpose that we ourselves do not have.

There is a desire among young people for integrity, honesty, an authentic kind of purpose for life. Where is this purpose to be found? I believe it is to be found in the Word of God, the Bible, the only infallible rule of faith in practice in a day of relativity. What does the Bible have to say about this purpose? It says four very simple things, if we were to capsule them and bring them into focus.

One of these things is that God created you in His image to lead a full, meaningful, purposeful life. Jesus said, "I'm come that you might have life and have it more abundantly." But then the Bible says a second thing. Simply stated—something's gone wrong. I know it. I see it in my own life. I'm sure you see it in yours. The Bible analyzes this thing and calls it sin, a term that's out of date today among some but a term that is as relevant as this morning's newspaper.

Sin. The Bible says all have sinned and have come short of the glory of God. That "all" includes me, that "all includes you.

I am reminded of a young preacher who was preaching a stem-winding sermon on sin. People were sort of stodgy and sleepy as he talked. He said, "Everyone in here is a sinner." Well, he didn't get any response on that. He tried it again. Still everybody was sort of sleepy-eyed. He figured he'd put it as a question: "Is there anyone here who's not sinned?" Well, he still didn't get much of a response. So he figured he'd use an even more personal direct question. He said, "Is there anyone here this morning who can stand up and say, 'I've never sinned?'" Just as he was ready to speed on with the sermon, not thinking anyone would take him up on the offer, he spotted a man about three-quarters of the way back, standing. Dumfounded, he stopped and asked, "Sir, are you standing?"

"Yes, I am standing."

"Well," he said, "did you hear my question?"

The man responded, "Yes, I heard your question."

The preacher said, "Are you sure you did? I asked, is there anyone here who has not sinned." The man said, "I heard your question and I'm standing."

"You mean you've never sinned?"

"No, I don't mean that. I'm standing on behalf of my wife's first husband."

You know and I know that there's something disjointed in life. Sin is not a grocery list of don'ts. Sin is a basic attitude of life in which you, in which I, try to run our own lives independent of God in Jesus Christ. That's what sin is, the Biblical definition of sin. All the other sins just filter down underneath that one main principle of ego running life—unsurrendered ego, unsurrendered to God.

But there's a third principle in the Scripture that's a terrific principle. It is that God sees us, the God out there, the God you see in nature, the God of the mountain scene or the sea scape, the God who also comes in terrible thunderstorms and hurricanes. We don't see God entirely in nature. We see one aspect of God. This God loves us. This God became a person in Jesus Christ, to die for your sins, to die for my sins. God was Christ reconciling all men unto Himself. This is the message, the purposeful, wonderful message of God's love for you. Jesus Christ died for your sins. Jesus Christ rose from the dead, literally, bodily rose from the dead to give you purpose for living.

But there's a fourth thing in the Word of God. Some of you may have gone as far as these first three, but the fourth is simply this. You need to receive Jesus Christ personally. "For God so loved the world." Yes, but God so loved you that if you give your life to Him, you shall not perish, but have eternal life in the here and the now. "But as many as received him," the Bible says, "to them gave he power to become the sons of God."

Well, you say, "I've thought about this and it sounds interesting. Someday I'll make a decision." It you've not already made a decision for Christ, you're sliding sideways. Dan Chandler, Vice President of Northeast Airlines, told me one time that there is in business the "do-nothing decision." It's a decision to do nothing and suffer the consequences of doing nothing. You've made a decision and therefore you have to pay the price of that decision to do nothing. It's the same thing in the Christian life. Not to make a decision to give your life to Jesus Christ implies you have not given your life to Jesus Christ. I invite you today to surrender yourselves, to let Jesus Christ come into your life and give you a purpose true for living.

God wants you, like Daniel, not only to have a purpose true but to be willing to make that purpose known. The Apostle Paul cried out in a great affirmation, "I am not ashamed of the gospel of Christ: for it is the power of God unto salvation."

Two nights ago my wife Anne and I went to see *Woodstock,* the movie that is so controversial. Now, I know the adult generation considers it an immoral film. There are a lot of things in it that I couldn't for a moment countenance. The day after we went, the Coral Gable City Commission closed the film down. The kids say that action was a double standard. I checked the newspaper. There are a couple of "skinflics" continuing to show in Coral Gables. The young people say, "Why are they picking on us when the adult generation won't grapple with its own sin?"

As we sat in the movie theater, we had to close our ears just to survive because the music was so loud. Some say our younger generation is going to be deaf with the bombardment of high decibels of music that we're getting today. There were only about five or six of us over twenty-five in the audience. The others weren't bothered by this noise.

But as we sat there, my mind flipped back to last summer. I'd flown from Miami to Boston to preach at Park Street Congregational Church. It was the weekend of Woodstock. I was in the taxi getting from the hotel to the church. And the taxicab driver, who was semi-longhaired, began to pepper me with questions when he learned that I was a minister. They were hostile questions. "Ah, this phoniness of religion! This hypocrisy! I wouldn't go to church!"

So we got to talking. I said, "I feel the same way you do."

He said, "What do you mean? You're a minister."

"Yes, but there is too much hypocrisy, and I see it in my own life." Then he began to open up and he said, "My, this is interesting."

We carried on a conversation for about ten minutes. Then it was time for me to get out of the cab and get in there and preach. I said, "Can you come to church?"

"No, I can't. I've got to work today. Are you preaching again here in Boston?"

I said, "Tonight."

Well, we left it at that. Much to my amazement that evening I looked down as I got up to preach. There was Bill the cab driver in the third row with his girl friend. He was the only long-haired fellow in the church.

After I'd preached he came up and asked, "Hey, how about coming over to my pad tonight, over on Beacon Street? We'll rap awhile. I've got some of my friends coming over."

I was exhausted after a long day, but it was a combination of ministerial responsibility and curiosity that led me to go over. I climbed five flights of stairs in a rickety old building and walked in. There were about twelve or so college kids, one Black Muslim, several what we call hippies, Bill and some of his friends of this middle-ground type. Until two in the morning we rapped.

The thing that amazed me was the integrity of these young people and the questing nature of their minds. They wanted to hear what I had to say. What is the Church really trying to say? Who is this Jesus Christ? Is he just someone for fancy dressed-up people in beautiful cathedrals, or is he someone who has something to say to me today where I live?

About twelve o'clock, a little gal wandered in, a cute little gal. She had just come back from Woodstock. She reported, "You know, I had a wonderful weekend. No phoniness, no sham." This was her idea of what had happened there.

Those kids taught me a lesson. The lesson is this: If we claim to be Christian men and women, if we claim to be a Christian nation, we have to have as part and parcel of our lives an integrity of personal commitment to Jesus Christ and also the willingness to share it with others. I think we suffer from sort of a CIA mentality, sort of a Secret Service attitude with our faith. Internal, meaningful maybe, yet we are scared to death even to share with someone else a testimony of what Jesus Christ means to us personally.

I don't mean to mingle religion and politics, church and state. No. Anyone can share a personal testimony of what Jesus Christ means to him without forcing it on anybody else. "Dare to have a purpose true;/Dare to make it known."

Then another thing in this little Sunday school song is simply "Dare to stand alone." The man who is God's man will, like Daniel, be willing to stand alone.

When I lived in Princeton my apartment overlooked the offices of the Gallup Poll. I used to look down from our window and see all the things going on in there, the gathering of information from around the world. I was there this week for a seminar and saw George Gallup, Jr., walking down the street. I've always been fascinated with pollsters. I must admit I've become a little bit cynical about polls. Now, I can do that. I'm a minister. I'm not subject to polls, as some of you here are.

The presidents in my lifetime, Roosevelt, Truman, Eisenhower, Kennedy, Johnson—I've watched them. Up and down the polls. What do we remember them for? The poll of a particular day? No. We remember them for what contribution they made when they were willing to stand alone. This doesn't mean you can't be popular and be a Christian. It does mean you can be freed from being driven by a desire for popularity—whether it's in elected office, whether it's as a secretary in an office, whether it's a subordinate in some phase of government. It doesn't mean you can't be loyal to your constituency and to your boss. It does mean you should be willing, with conviction and character, to have a primary commitment to Jesus Christ—a commitment that gives you the freedom of being an honest servant of God and of the people, with an individual integrity.

Daniel found that this quality endeared him to some who didn't share his faith, because they could trust him as a servant of God and a servant of the state. He was willing to stand alone. The man who is a courageous Christian leader will have to stand alone. He'll be caught between East and West, North and South, cold war and hot war, compromising withdrawal or immoral carnage. There are grays here. It's impossible to distinguish the black and the white in so many of our contemporary issues. But that man will claim the strength of God who has the courage to stand alone.

One day in this White House, March 19, 1920, Woodrow Wilson lay stretched out sick in the Lincoln bed. The Senate had just that day come to the conclusion that the United States would not enter the League of Nations. This man was heartbroken as he lay there in his bed. The hours ticked by. Midnight came. It was the 20th of March. At three o'clock in the morning, still sleepless, Woodrow Wilson called out to his doctor, Admiral Cary Grayson. "Doctor," he said, "get me my Bible, get me my Bible and turn to Second Corinthians, Chapter Four, verses eight and nine."

Grayson brought the Bible to the President and began to read these words: "We are troubled on every side, yet not distressed; we are perplexed, but not in despair; persecuted, but not forsaken; cast down, but not destroyed. . . ."

The man of God with a purpose true, who is willing to let it be known, is a man who dares to stand alone. When he's alone he has this kind of confidence—confidence in the presence of Jesus Christ to help him, to strengthen him.

I challenge you this morning to: "Dare to be a Daniel;/Dare to stand alone;/Dare to have a purpose true;/And dare to make it known."

# May 10, 1970

Prelude

Opening Remarks                                THE PRESIDENT

Doxology

Prayer                    THE REVEREND STEPHEN T. SZILAGYI
                   Pastor, Philippus United Church of Christ
                                            Cincinnati, Ohio
                         Chaplain of the American Legion
                                         Department of Ohio

Anthem                    THE CALVIN THEOLOGICAL SEMINARY
                                                      CHOIR
                                    Grand Rapids, Michigan
               *"An Anthem of Penitence, Pardon and Peace"*
                            compiled by Herbert A. Start

Hymn                       *"What a Friend We Have in Jesus"*

Sermon                                     *"With Gratitude"*

Anthem                    THE CALVIN THEOLOGICAL SEMINARY
                                                      CHOIR
         *"Precious Lord, Take My Hand"* by George N. Allen

Benediction

Postlude


Singing this morning are members of the Calvin Theological Seminary Choir from Grand Rapids, Michigan. This group includes 24 men, all of whom are
preparing to enter the ministry of the Christian Re-
formed Church. Mr. Herbert A. Start is director of the
choir.

# The Reverend Stephen T. Szilagyi

THE PRESIDENT: As most of you who have attended these Worship Services in the White House know, we have tried to make them ecumenical, and we are also trying to make them geographical in terms of covering the country.

After having a very splendid choir from up in New York State a couple of weeks ago, I had a call from Congressman Gerald Ford. He asked, "Have you forgotten Calvin Theological Seminary?" I said, "No." Certainly, *he* hadn't forgotten it.

I remembered my visit to Calvin some time ago, and I also recalled that it was one of the outstanding college choirs in all the United States. We are delighted that, through Congressman Ford, this fine singing group was able to come to Washington to provide our musical worship this morning.

We have had ministers from California and from Florida, from the Northeast and the West and the South. I thought I'd covered the country reasonably well until I got a call from Senator Saxbe of Ohio, who pointed out that there was a young minister in Cincinnati, the pastor of the Philippus United Church of Christ in Cincinnati, who really should be invited. So, he is here today. He has, moreover, a background that I think all of us would be interested in knowing about. The Reverend Mr. Szilagyi was born in Czechoslovakia, but his parents were Hungarian. He came to the United States in 1952, and is now a proud citizen of this country. And we, of course, are proud to have him as a citizen, just as we are proud of so many of the millions of Americans who

167

have come here from other countries. He is now also the Chaplain of the American Legion in the State of Ohio.

THE REVEREND MR. SZILAGYI: Eternal and ever-blessed God, as we walk the ways of life, there are so many things which we must meet. Help us to meet them right. Help us to meet temptation with resistance and never feebly, without struggle, to surrender to the wrong things. Help us to meet disappointment with acceptance and never to waste time in vainly longing for the things which are not for us. Help us to meet difficulty with perseverance, and never to surrender to defeat because a task is hard to do, or a problem is hard to solve. Help us to meet work with diligence, and never to offer anyone that which is less than our best. Help us to meet injury and insult with forgiveness, and never to allow a long, embittered resentment to reign within our hearts. Help us to meet worry with serenity, and never to lose our confidence and our calm. Help us to meet sorrow with trust, and never to sorrow as if there were no hope.

Help us to meet the appeal to help with graciousness, and never to grudge to give that which it is in our power to give. Help us to meet the call to service with eagerness, and never to be selfishly lost in our own concerns. Help us to meet life with courage, and death without fear, because we meet all things with thee.

Help us to be more devoted to our great country, and strive to make it even greater through our efforts. Help us to be more grateful for our men in uniform, and for the service they perform for the sake of freedom. Help us to be aware of the immensity of the problems which face our beloved President, a sincere and dedicated leader, who has inherited war but who seeks a world at peace. Bless the home, the church, and our beloved America with thy constant presence and love. Hear this prayer for thy love's sake, we ask. Amen.

The text of our message today is from the Book of Proverbs, the 31st Chapter, the 28th verse: "Her children rise up and call her blessed."

My dear brethren in Christ, there is a legend that God sent an angel down from heaven to find the most beautiful thing on this earth and bring it back to heaven. When the angel saw the flowers in springtime, he said, "These must be the most beautiful things on earth," and he gathered them up in a beautiful bouquet to take them back to heaven. Then he met a child of wondrous beauty and golden hair and a lovely smile; and when he saw that child, he said, "This must be the most wondrous thing on earth. Nothing could ever be sweeter than this child. Nothing could be sweeter than the smile on that innocent child's face."

But farther along in a remote valley, he came to a humble cottage where a mother sat in a doorway with a little babe in her lap. And as he watched her tender and beautiful care for the little babe, he said, "This must be the fairest thing on earth. I will take back mother's love with me to heaven."

When he reached the gates of heaven, the flowers had faded and had died. The smile on the child's face had changed to a frown. But the mother's love was unchanged.

There are those among you who recall your own godly fathers and mothers. You never think of them in terms of money, whether they left you much or little or nothing at all in material wealth. If they left you the imprint of their character and prayers, that is an inheritance incorruptible, undefiled; and it fadeth not away. The money which they left you may have disappeared long ago, but the influence of their godly example is an ever-present reality and power. Of all the men I have known, I cannot recall one man who turned out well, whose mother did not do her level best for him when he was a little child.

This world of ours can get along well without well-dressed ladies, but it will perish without devoted, dedicated, loving mothers; for the mothers of yesterday made today what today is; and the mothers of today will establish the future of the world. And the child—if he reacts in a positive way, and if he is a contribution to the world, it is because of a good home and a good mother. If he reacts in a negative way, it is because there was no contribution from that home and from that mother.

My friends, no doubt you have heard the following story many times, but let us examine it once more. The story is about the ten lepers that were healed by Jesus. But as you might remember the story, after the ten lepers were healed, they went their way, and only one out of the ten returned to thank the Lord. I wonder what happened to the other nine who were healed.

Let us look at the story and perhaps we might see the inside of this. We might see what happened. Let us examine them individually. The first one might have been lazy. He might have said to himself, "I will come back later. No doubt, I will see the Lord again and I will thank him; or perhaps at a later time, I might send him a thank-you note or card." This man did not understand the virtue of gratitude.

The second one might have been a cynic. "Why shouldn't he help me? We all know that he is a preacher and a healer, and that is his job to help people. He did his duty to me and that was all. He did what he was supposed to do." This one was too dumb to be sensitive. He did not understand that people such as Christ, who care about others, are sensitive people. Sensitive people help and care because they are concerned; because they love and they care. And Christ would have loved to hear from this man. He would have loved to receive just a simple thank-you note or simple thank-you response.

The third one might have been hateful. "The reason why he healed me—well, because he could not stand the sight of me the way I was. All others avoided me. He was just like they are."

Then came the suspicious one. "It was my lucky day. I was at the right place at the right time. That is the way it is. If he had not cured me or healed me, someone else would have done it some other time at some other place."

Then came the fifth one, the one with the superior attitude. "I owe him nothing. The Nazarene who cured me is nothing more than a poor peasant. Why should I thank him? He's below my station in life. I'm too intelligent, too good." His superior attitude, his pride, would not allow him to be grateful. Have you ever seen people like that in life? No doubt you have.

Then came the scheming type. "Why did he do it? What was in it for him? What did he want? What was his reason? What will he get out of it? If I had come back, he might have asked me for a donation or something."

Then there was the "loner." Jesus knew the type, and you know the type. "My religion is the best, my house, my children, anything that I have is the best." He was intolerant of Jesus, who in his mind was of a lower class than he himself.

Then came the eighth one, who had parts of all the attitudes of all those involved.

And the ninth one, of course could have been any one of us. How would you define him?

But the tenth one came back. He was sensitive. He was appreciative.

I told you the story about the ten lepers to clarify and emphasize a very true point of life: This has been true since the beginning of history; since the beginning of time—man's ingratitude to man and man's ingratitude to God; man's lack of appreciation for what he has, and man's lack of response in gratitude for what he has.

Gratitude is a very natural thing in life, but we must allow it to come out. We must let it grow. We must respond to God's generosity. We must respond to man's goodness. It is also "blessed to receive" with an attitude of humility and gratitude; receive and respond with gratitude.

On this Mother's Day we remember the one great gift of mother. The word "Mother" has a special ring to it. Poems and books have been written about mother. Great men, upon reaching their greatest goal, expressed their gratitude to their mothers. Christ honored and respected his mother, and looked after her welfare even after he was gone. When General Grant's mother died, he said to the minister who was to officiate at the funeral, "Make no reference to me. She owed nothing to me at any post I occupied. Speak of her just as she was, a pure-minded, simplehearted, earnest Christian."

My friends, I heard a French legend one time about a young man, a somewhat foolish young man, who met a woman of somewhat questionable character. And she made a strange request of him. She said, "For you to prove your love to me, bring me your mother's heart, so I can feed it to my little dog." And the foolish young man responded. And as he was carrying his mother's heart, he fell and the heart dropped out of his hands. Then the heart spoke up, spoke to the son, this heart that he cut out to give to this woman's dog, and said, "Did you hurt yourself, my son?" This is mother's love. This is the deep love that a true mother possesses.

I heard another story from my grandmother, of a young man about nineteen years old, who was condemned to death by hanging for a very serious crime. His last request was that he wanted to see his mother. And they brought his mother to him. They expected a very tearful farewell—a son who is to die in a few minutes, with his loving and beloved mother. Yet the response was completely shocking to all those present. When he came and embraced his mother, he bit her ear off. And when they asked him why he did this, he said: "Mother, you put the noose around my neck. When I was little, and I did something bad, you said it was all right. When I acted in a bad way, you made excuses for me. You might as well have put the noose around my neck."

A mother's way is reflected in her children's lives. It was a mother who carried us in her womb. It was a mother who taught us to speak. It was a mother who taught us to pray. It was a mother who taught us to love with her own love, a constant display of love and care on a mother's part. And, as I said, she taught us to speak. And, do you know, the strangest thing is this: that even though she taught us to speak, yet usually the first word a child speaks is not "Mother," but "Daddy." Love shining through—shining through and through!

When Alexander the Great entertained the kings and nobles of the courts of Persia, he appeared wearing only those garments which had been entirely made for him by his mother. Long ago, we have discarded the garments which were made by the loving hands of our mothers, and yet, in a certain sense, as to life and character, we are all still wearing the garments which were woven for us by our mothers. Anything that is beautiful, kind, and loving in this world, no doubt, mother had something to do with it.

On one occasion, my oldest son, when he was five and one-half, as might be very typical for a minister's son, was on a "sermon kick." And so, as I was babysitting with the children, he said, "Daddy, I'm going to deliver a sermon to you." I said, "Fine, son, fine." And then, wanting to assert my parental influence on him just a little bit more, I said, "Son, why don't you tell us how to be good, obey God, and listen to our parents?"

His response shocked me. He said, "Daddy, the preacher says and does whatever he wants to say and do." I thought to myself that he had a lot to learn. No one in life does those things. And then he proceeded to deliver his sermon. He said that God is good, and God is great; He loves us and we love Him; He understands us and we understand Him; *"but we do whatever we want to do anyway."* And all this time, his three-and-one-half-year-old sister was sitting in a rocking chair, rocking back and forth; and every once in awhile she came forth with this comment: "You are right, Georgie, you are right."

This is the way it is in life. I can see on your faces, in my own congregation, or speaking in front of any group, that there are responses, nods of the heads. On one occasion I delivered a message in a church, when all of a sudden, someone in the congregation said, "Amen." It shocked me. But realizing that he was agreeing with me, I repeated the same sentence over again, and he came back with another "Amen" and two more joined him. Soon I was getting these "Amens" left and right. After I got through, the minister from the church said to me, "Your sermon rated very high. You received about twenty-four 'Amens.' This is an excellent rating for a sermon."

This is the way it is. And I would have one request to make of you: Don't nod your heads in approval, but be liberal with what your mother taught you; that is, give of yourself to God and to man and to country in love; but be also strong in your faith; be strong in your life. Give not away your God. Give not away your country to those who would toss it aside and give it to others. In these ways, by showing strength, express your gratitude to your mother.

I can't seem to keep my children out of my sermons. Again, it was my oldest son. Our dog was hit by a car, and in this sad experience, we thought we would teach our son a lesson for life. If the dog were to live, the boy would learn about the possibilities of recovery, and have gratitude in his heart that his prayers were answered. In the event that the dog were to die, then he would learn about death. So, as we were taking this little dog in the back seat of our car to the veterinarian, and the boy was sitting in the back seat with the dog, and trying to comfort the dog, and pray for the dog, suddenly the most surprising thing came out of him. He said, "Sweetie," which was the dog's name, "I wish it was me instead of you."

What a good attitude that would be for us to take in behalf of our fellow man! When I heard him say this and act in this way, I knew that his mother was coming through. My friends, is your mother coming through in your life?

"Her children rise up and call her blessed; her husband also, and he praises her." Many women have done excellently, but you surpassed them all, Mother.

We have a good friend in the Cincinnati area, a newspaper-woman, school administrator, author of three books, one of which I have just presented to President Nixon for his library. Her name is Alice Kennelly Roberts. In this book, *Bluegrass Sea-*

*sons*, she has written a poem called, "A Mother Speaks," which seems to express the true feeling of a mother's heart about her son. It seems appropriate to include it in this Mother's Day sermon.

Time spins a magic web of dreams
    Across the crowded years,
I see a host of yesterdays—
    Shadows of smiles and tears.
My heart remembers still the pain,
    Surmounted soon by joy,
In knowing God had shared with me
    A precious baby boy.

I rocked you softly to and fro
    Through lazy summer days,
And pressed you close against my heart
    And soothed your restless ways.
Your eyes were wide and soft and blue,
    Reflecting trust and love,
And as I hummed a lullaby,
    I prayed to God above.

The months went by. You learned to speak;
    And, kneeling by your bed,
I heard in reverent humbleness
    The first prayer that you said.
Your baby steps soon followed me
    Wherever I would go,
And when you fell, I suffered more
    Than you will ever know.

Then came the day we had to bow
    To education's rule;
I caught the tear you didn't see,
    And sent you off—to school.

The years went by. You had your quarrels;
  And mother's heart would yearn
To shield your bruises and your pain,
  But knew you had to learn.

On graduation day, I stood
  Beside your happy Dad
And knew the glow of pride he felt—
  The only son we had.
It wasn't long 'til war came on;
  The country needed men.
My frightened heart stood still, I know,
  Then gave you up again.

Each night I wondered where you camped,
  And prayed most earnestly
That He who gave His only Son
  Would give mine back to me.
And finally the day arrived—
  The war you fought was won!
I clasped you to my breast once more,
  The man who was my son.

You married soon—a lovely girl;
  And yet, somehow I knew
A vague and empty loneliness
  At seeing her with you.
But when your little son was born,
  With eyes so soft and blue,
I cradled in my arms again
  The baby that was you.

He snuggled softly at my breast
  As you had often done,
And then I knew it was for this
  That I had shared my son.

And so, I rocked him to and fro,
  And prayed a silent prayer
That God should take your little son
  Into His loving care.

And as I pressed him to my heart
  And soothed his restless ways,
I saw across the crowded years
  A host of yesterdays;
My heart remembered still the pain—
  The evil and the good;
But God had given me his best
  In precious Motherhood!

## September 13, 1970

Prelude

Opening Remarks          THE PRESIDENT

Prayer        THE HONORABLE BROOKS HAYS
Co-Chairman, Former Members of Congress, Inc.

Doxology

Scriptural Reading     THE HONORABLE BROOKS HAYS

Anthem       THE ALL-PHILADELPHIA BOYS CHOIR
PHILADELPHIA, PENNSYLVANIA
*"O Come, Let Us Sing Unto The Lord"* (Psalm 95:1-3)
Kent A. Newbury
*"Ole Ark's A-Moverin' "* (Negro Spiritual)
Arranged: Hamilton

Sermon       THE HONORABLE WALTER H. JUDD
Co-Chairman, Former Members of Congress, Inc.
*"Are God's Laws Relevant Today?"*

Anthem       THE ALL-PHILADELPHIA BOYS CHOIR
*"Cantate Domino (O Sing unto the Lord)"*
Hassler (1564-1612)
*"Ride the Chariot"* (Negro Spiritual)
Arranged: Hamilton

Benediction     *"The Lord Bless You and Keep You"*

Postlude

# The Honorable Walter H. Judd

THE PRESIDENT: We're very honored this morning to welcome the members of the organization Former Members of Congress to this White House Worship Service.

For the musical part of the service, we have a very fine organization that I had the privilege of hearing before they took off for a trip to Europe, including two appearances in the Soviet Union, in Leningrad and Moscow: the All-Philadelphia Boys Choir.

Presiding over our Worship Service are two former members of the House of Representatives. Most of us here will remember them, and many of us know them personally. They are: Brooks Hays from Arkansas, who served for sixteen years in the House and who had an unprecedented two terms as a layman head of the Southern Baptist Convention; and Walter Judd of Minnesota, who served for twenty years in the House and who, before he went to the House of Representatives, was a medical missionary in China.

THE HONORABLE MR. HAYS: Our Father, one of our principle purposes in this assembly is to renew the commitments to thy law made by our forefathers. We believe these commitments account for whatever divinity there is in our public life. This is our corporate prayer, but as individuals we cry out as thy creatures, with all the frailties of human-kind, for a new consciousness of thee. May the restlessness of our souls, which we know will not cease until we rest in thee, meanwhile propel us willingly and devotedly into life's duties, filled with confidence that this world is still in thy hands.

We pray for the President and for his family. None know better than we, his guests today, the weight of his burdens. These he cannot cast away. But we ask that they may be accompanied by an awareness of thy presence and thy help. More than for ourselves, we ask thy protecting care for the country we love. We know that thou art the judge of all nations and the Father of all peoples. We would therefore ask for nothing that we would not share with others, wherever they are, whatever their status.

We pray that we may be instruments of thy will in the distraught world which desperately needs thy guidance and thy peace. This we can do with firmness in the right as thou hast given us to see the right. We cannot be blind to the unleashed forces that are contrary to thy laws, the cruelties and the imperfections which we long to see vanish from this earth. All of our hopes would be in vain without thee. We cannot understand it, but we accept as truth the Bible's assurance that thou will be at our side in every struggle and will share our sufferings. This is our firm buttress against every peril. We pray it in Jesus' name and in His spirit. Amen.

THE HONORABLE MR. JUDD: Mr. President, Mrs. Nixon, friends, fellow Americans. First, I want to join Brooks in expressing for all of the former Members of Congress our appreciation of the honor you do us today in inviting us to join you and your family, and your official family, in this service of worship at the White House.

Over two hundred former Members of Congress have joined this organization in the seven months since it was established, with the original suggestion coming from the gentleman from Arkansas, Mr. Hays. You will permit me to comment that this organization has a unique advantage over many in that it is certain to have a new group of persons eligible for membership every two years. It has a guaranteed clientele!

We hope that this association will enable those of us who have been in the Congress, the House or the Senate—with a few like yourself, Mr. President, graduates of both bodies—to continue the fellowship and close friendships developed in our years of working together on Capitol Hill. Perhaps it will also enable us to keep a little closer to affairs of state. We don't now have direct responsibilities for lawmaking, but there is no lessening of our concern for the well-being of this country. And especially in times as troubled as these.

No one will deny, I think, that we are living in a period characterized by as great a mixture of emotions as any in our nation's history. On one hand, never did anybody have so much to be grateful for, and I'm sure most Americans are deeply thankful for the goodness of living and the freedoms that are possible for us here. But at the same time, there's never been greater uneasiness, uncertainty, dismay, perplexity, approaching in many instances, anxiety. Everywhere there are conflicts.

Abroad, for the first time in history, there are conflicts on all continents at the same time.

And there are widespread conflicts here at home. We've been accustomed to assassinations, insurrections, riots, disorders in other countries, but have assumed that in the United States things would always be stable. And now we see deep questioning in our country, both of the values on which the nation was founded and grew great, and of our basic institutions, especially among our youth.

There is the criticism that we haven't lived up to the values we profess. And at the other extreme there is an assault upon the values themselves—the contention that they aren't essential or necessarily good, even if we do live up to them. They are said to be just ancient preachments that don't apply to our times.

Equally there's widespread questioning of our basic institutions.

First, of our political institutions. Questioning of all of them, including our own Alma Mater, the Congress, not to mention the Judiciary, and even occasionally, some questions about one department or another of the Executive branch!

Questioning of our economic institutions, the means by which goods and services are produced and distributed—the market-place.

Questioning of our educational institutions at all levels—the school.

Questioning of our social institutions, beginning with the most basic of all, the home.

And questioning of our religious institutions—the temple. Are the Judeo-Christian faith, hertage, body of ethics, on which this nation was established relevant to us, suitable or adequate for such times as these? Or is God dead? Or never was?

Surely it was never more urgent that we in America take our bearings afresh. *Is* there a moral order in the universe?

There's an astronomical order; nobody doubts that. Our astronauts wouldn't have moved one foot into space if they hadn't been absolutely sure there is an order out there. We don't know too much about it yet. Our job is to find out what it is, what its laws are and live *with* them instead of against them.

No one denies there is a physical order. It isn't said we ought to try to create a chemical order for our times or a biological order.

But is there or is there not an order in that realm which is most important of all: the relation of people to people—a moral order? An order like the others whose laws man can violate but which he cannot break, because they're in the nature of things.

*Are* there any fundamental principles or laws that are universal, that are always true in every age and in every place—

That apply to *all* peoples, *all* races, *all* classes, *all* nations;
to the rich and to the poor;
to the employer and to the employee;
to the majority and to the minority?
If so, what are those principles or laws?

By what standards are we to judge proposals that come from this, that, or the other source? By what yardsticks are we to measure progress or decay, good or bad?

How can we in America make a united nation again out of our deeply divided people?

How can we build a united world out of the divided peoples and nations on this dangerously contracted planet?

Perhaps we can get some guidance from the experience of those who have gone through troubled times in the past. I'd like to use as our example this morning the children of Israel.

When Moses led them out of Egypt where they had been four hundred years in captivity, they had deep family ties, tribal ties, blood ties, and they had strong religious ties. But they hadn't developed political ties. They hadn't had opportunity to develop them; the Pharoahs had made all those decisions for them, and it takes time and experience to develop political consciousness, and skill in establishing the institutions and laws under which people can live together in harmony and peace.

How could Moses weld this collection of tribes and families into a political organism, able to hold its own and deal successfully with its own people and with its neighbors?

How make a nation out of a people?

You will recall that Moses, wrestling with this task, went up into a mountain alone where God gave him—or helped him work out —ten great fundamental principles or laws for Israel. Our forefathers believed in these and sought to apply them, live by them. My question this morning is, are they relevant for us today, our nation, our world, our times?

The longer I served in government, and especially after I had yielded, or seen some of my colleagues yield, to the temptation to try short cuts or expediencies that violated these laws, the more convinced I became that there are none better for us. In fact —I will say it more strongly—I doubt that there are any others on which, as a base, we can build a society, a nation, that will endure and prosper.

So first let me just run through them, reminding you of each with a sentence or two, and then try to see if they have relevance for us today. And always interpreting them here today from this standpoint only: nation-building.

The first, of course, is that God must be at the center of things. To put one's race at the center, ancestry, class, party, work, even one's own family, certainly one's self, divides. Not power or position or prestige, but GOD must be at the center, or things just won't go right. Not because God is self-seeking, but because He wants us not to make the fatal mistake of putting something else *at the center*. THOU SHALT HAVE NO OTHER GODS BEFORE ME.

The second is the same law, said negatively—the folly and the futility of putting one's main trust in things. Because things *at the center* will fail you. That which can be possessed can be lost, and then what do you have? THOU SHALT NOT MAKE UNTO THEE ANY GRAVEN IMAGE.

The third is the sacredness of the Divine-Human fellowship. One cannot have God at the center if that relationship is profaned or exploited or trifled with or used for selfish purposes. It alienates one from God. THOU SHALT NOT TAKE THE NAME OF THE LORD THY GOD IN VAIN.

The fourth is the claim of God on a portion of our time. This is the positive requirement. You can't develop a close relationship with the woman you love enough to ask to be your wife unless you give time, thought, and attention to it—and to her. Do we imagine we can develop a close, intimate fellowship with God, so we can have Him at the center, can know His will and lay hold on His resources that are available for us, if we don't give time to it—and to Him? The Sabbath is a symbol of this claim of God on a portion of our time, our substance, our lives, ourselves. REMEMBER THE SABBATH DAY TO KEEP IT HOLY.

The fifth is the sacredness of the home, the family, which has been the pattern of organization of every good and stable society all down through the centuries. Jesus so often took these ancient precepts or laws and reaffirmed them, lifted them up, lived by them. On the cross, in almost the last hour of his life, he made provision for his mother. Seeing her and the beloved disciple, he said to her, "Behold thy Son." And to the disciple, "Behold thy Mother." No enduring society has been or can be built in which the home is not a holy and sacred institution. HONOR THY FATHER AND THY MOTHER. Not just counsel—*law*.

The sixth is the sacredness of human life. It's really more than we ordinarily mean by that, I think, as I learned once when studying Chinese. Sometimes I read the Bible with my teacher because I thought I knew what it meant and all I had to do was to learn how to say it in Chinese. One day when we were reading the Commandments, my teacher, a courtly Confucian gentleman, said somewhat diffidently, "I once heard one of you Christian preachers talk about his Commandment and he interpreted it as if it meant only, Thou shalt not kill *the body*. But it doesn't say that. It says, Thou shalt not *kill*." He added, "We Chinese think it's worse to kill or crush the human spirit than it is to kill the body. And your own leader said, 'Don't be afraid of those who can kill the body but cannot kill the spirit.' "

Mrs. Judd and I just got back two weeks ago from the Soviet Union. The thing that most disturbs one there is the obvious crushing, subjugation, of the human spirit. It's the whole human person that's sacred; not just the body. Lawless, capricious destruction of human persons makes impossible the building of a good society.THOU SHALT NOT KILL—the body or the spirit.

The seventh is the sacredness of the sex relations in the bonds of matrimony. Of course, anything as intimate and personal as sex relations ought to be sacred under any circumstances, because promiscuity cheapens. But especially in matrimony must they be sacred because if they're not, then the home breaks, and the nation deteriorates. This is not a matter of arbitrary rules; it's a matter of moral law. I'll say it more strongly—of social necessity if the nation is to stand. THOU SHALT NOT COMMIT ADULTERY.

The next is the sacredness of property. First, of the other person's property—the obligation not to take what belongs to

someone else. But that's not all. The sacredness of one's own
property—the obligation to use it is a sacred trust in terms of the
well-being of people—and of the community. THOU SHALT NOT
STEAL—from man, or from God.

The ninth also is a double one. First, the sacredness of reputation. All who have been in public life understand the cruelty of
slander or innuendo. Shakespeare put it:

> Who steals my purse steals trash; . . .
> But he that filches from me my good name
> Robs me of that which not enriches him
> And makes me poor indeed.

It means also the sacredness of the pledged word. Surely
there's no hope of a decent world of order and justice and
peace unless the pledged word of men and nations can be
trusted. THOU SHALT NOT BEAR FALSE WITNESS.

And the tenth comes around full circle to the first again: the
menace of an unsound heart. The menace to society and the
menace to the one who has it. For at the center is covetousness,
self, a cancer, instead of *God*. THOU SHALT NOT COVET.

Now here are the ten fundamental laws that God helped Moses
work out for Israel. Increasingly I believe they are God's unchanging laws for us too—and for other peoples.

But it isn't enough to get laws, to enact them, or define them
or interpret them; we must apply them. We have to live by them.

Moses, you recall, came down from the mountain, exulting. His
face shone. Now he had the answers to the problem of making
a nation out of a people. And what did he find? While he'd been
gone, some of the people had murmured, "We don't know what's
happened to that Moses. We've got to have something concrete,
tangible, to put our trust in; something we can see and touch."
So they had made them a golden calf as their god. Oh, they didn't
ask anybody else to do it for them. They chipped in their own

rings and bracelets, they made their own contributions to provide themselves security. And they were dancing around the golden calf for joy.

And what did Moses do? Like most of us under strain, he broke, lost his temper, "cast the tables out of his hands, and brake them beneath the mount." And he said, "Who is on the Lord's side? Let him come unto me." And the sons of Levi, one tribe, came over and they set to and slaughtered some three thousand of their brethren, broke some of the very laws that were to be the foundation of the nation.

Then Moses had a bad night. In the morning, like a father yearning over a wayward child, he went out alone again, and he said, "Oh, this people have sinned a great sin, and have made them gods of gold." (Can you think of any other people of whom that might be said?) "Yet now, if thou wilt forgive their sin—; and if not, blot me, I pray thee, out of thy book which thou hast written." If my people have to go down, I don't ask to be spared. I go down with them. But if thou wilt—give us another chance.

What did the Lord say? And now we come to the application to ourselves. He said to Moses, "Hew thee two tables of stone like unto the first." That is, Go right back where you got off the track and get on the track.

"And I will write upon these tables the words that were in the first tables, which thou brakest." The same words, the same unchanging laws of God—for them, for us, for the universe.

The same laws of character-building, of home-building, of community-building, of nation-building, of peace-building. God's eternal laws.

The same words as given to Moses 4,000 years ago. The same words as reaffirmed and amplified by Jesus two thousand years ago. The same words, in substance, as in the Mayflower Compact and the Declaration of Independence and our Constitution. The same words, principles, laws. No man or nation is going to get around God.

And the Lord said to Moses, "Be ready in the morning." That is, Don't fool around about this, Moses, get at it.

"And come up in the morning unto mount Sinai." Come UP. Life never was coasting. It's always been climbing. That's not a curse, it's a blessing—UP.

"And present thyself there to me in the top of the mount." Not at the bottom of the mountain, that's not good enough. Not the middle of the mountain, that's not good enough. But in the *top* of the mountain—where we see most clearly and surely what is true and fundamental and everlasting.

"And *present* thyself there to me. . . ." Not just discussion and debate, but commitment, dedication.

"And no man shall come up with thee." Every nation as well as every man must have its reckoning with the Almighty.

And we read:

"And he hewed two tables of stone like unto the first; and Moses rose up early in the morning, and went up unto mount Sinai, as the Lord had commanded him, and took in his hands the two tables of stone." That is, he obeyed.

"And the Lord descended in the cloud, and stood with him there." He always does *when we obey.*

"And Moses made haste, and bowed his head toward the earth, and worshipped. And he said, If now I have found grace in thy sight, O Lord, let my Lord, I pray thee, go among us; for it is a stiffnecked people; and pardon our iniquity and our sin, and take us for thine inheritance."

Blessed was our nation when its God was the Lord. Blessed again, and always, will be our nation—and every nation—when its God is the Lord.

> Lord God of Hosts,
> Be with us yet,
> Lest we forget!
> Lest we forget!

## October 18, 1970

Prelude

Opening Remarks                                 THE PRESIDENT

Prayer                                          JOHN ERICKSON

Doxology

Scriptural Reading                                    REX KERN

Anthem                                THE DANISH BOYS' CHOIR
                                         Selected Danish Hymns

Sermon                                     BOBBY RICHARDSON

Anthem                                THE DANISH BOYS' CHOIR
                                  *"Let There Be Peace on Earth"*
                                     Sy Miller and Jill Jackson

Benediction                                    JAY WILKINSON

Postlude

The Danish Boys' Choir is attached to the Danish
Broadcasting System and performs monthly on
television. The choir includes 20 members between
the ages of 10 and 14. The boys do not go to the same
school, but meet twice a week in Copenhagen for
rehearsals and practice. This is their second visit to
the United States, and their tour will include both the
east and west coasts. Directing the choir is Mr. Hen-
ning Elbirk.

# Bobby Richardson

THE PRESIDENT: As always, we are delighted to have all of you here as our guests at this White House Worship Service, and we think we have a highly unusual program this morning. This time, instead of asking some distinguished member of the clergy to conduct our service, we have turned to the world of sports.

The four men participating in the program either are or have been prominent sports figures. They are all members, or have been members, of the Fellowship of Christian Athletes—an organization whose purpose is to confront athletes and coaches, and through them the youth of the nation, with the challenge and adventure of following Christ in the followship of the Church. The FCA reaches all levels in the field of sports—high school, college, and professional athletes and coaches.

John Erickson, who will offer the opening prayer at this service, was head basketball coach at the University of Wisconsin for nine years and has served on the advisory board of FCA. Rex Kern, who gives the Scripture reading, is a senior at Ohio State and plays quarterback for the Buckeyes. He is an active member of FCA. Jay Wilkinson, formerly of the White House staff, was an active participant in FCA during his football-playing days at Duke University. He will give our benediction today.

And of course Bobby Richardson, who will give us our sermon, is such a bright name in the sports world that it is hardly necessary to review his career. I *will* mention, however, that he played spectacular baseball as second baseman for the New York Yankees in the days when they were an almost invincible ball club. He is now head baseball coach at the University of South Carolina —and is national representative for the Fellowship of Christian Athletes.

We are of course delighted to have all four of these men with us today. And we are also greatly pleased that a famous singing organization is here to round out this remarkable service. The Danish Boys' Choir is composed of twenty members between the ages of ten and fourteen. It is attached to the Danish Broadcasting System and performs regularly on television. It is now on a coast-to-coast tour of the United States, and we are fortunate that the choir could be with us here in the White House this morning.

MR. ERICKSON: Our Father, who art in heaven, as our heads are bowed and the activity within us is at rest, our hearts and our thoughts and all we have are turned over to thee in prayer and admiration. As we sometimes stumble through life, we often forget that your love is everlasting and your concern greater than we can ever imagine. For this, we are eternally grateful.

Continue to be with those who lead nations in roles of government; somehow instill in each a sense of inner strength that comes only from you. We thank you for men who commit themselves to your ways in their earthly lives and duties. We pray in particular for our President and his family and for all in roles of government in these United States who work unendingly for peace on earth.

We beseech thee, Lord, especially to bless the youth of our world. Show them the discipline by which life can be beautifully lived and character achieved. For those who use their bodies in physical activity and competition, keeping them as temples for your kingdom, we do humbly pray in thanksgiving.

And now, Oh Lord, we confess our many failures and weaknesses. Help us to accept your forgiveness and your great understanding. And create in each of us a desire to live for thee in all the days that follow. All this we ask in thy great name. Amen.

MR. RICHARDSON: Some years ago, I played in a baseball game at Los Angeles, and there were about 90,000 people in the stands. It was a benefit game for Roy Campanella, and there was real excitement at this ball game. I have played in over thirty World Series games, and there's always excitement there. But there's excitement here today, too, and even more than excitement, there is honor.

Mr. President, I thank you for the privilege of being here today and participating in this program. Because my profession and background is baseball and because I am not an ordained clergyman, I do not always feel at home behind a pulpit. I do feel comfortable here today, Mr. President, because I know the Quakers have no ordained clergy but in Christian humility share their faith and experience with each other under the guidance of God's spirit. And I am glad to share my faith here today.

This is a sports-oriented society we live in. I would bet that almost everybody in this room turned on his television set yesterday and watched the outcome of some of the football games around the country. And this past week, we've had the World Series, with the Baltimore Orioles playing the Cincinnati Reds. Basketball season has already started, and I was talking with John Erickson just a moment ago about the Atlanta Hawks playing the Bucks. I emphasize that this is truly a sports-oriented society that we live in, and I'm excited because I believe that the Fellowship of Christian Athletes can be one of the greatest exponents of the Christian witness in our land today.

I think one of the reasons that I can say this is because of their goal. Their goal is, very simply, that Christian athletes can and should band together with the idea of winning and influencing young boys to Christ. Their hope is to challenge athletes, and, through them, the youth of the nation, with the adventure of following Christ in the fellowship of the Church. And I am glad that Mr. Jim Jeffrey, who is the Executive Director of the Fellowship of Christian Athletes, and also some of the board of directors are here today. They are some of the men that make this organization go. And I'm glad to represent them as an athlete and as a Christian.

Some time ago I heard a person get up to speak, and he was sort of like I am now—quite nervous. He was given a very fine introduction, but there were tears in his eyes as he rose to speak. Finally he said, "I had some prepared notes of a speech that I wanted to give here today, but I'd like to put these aside and share something with you. It all started ten years ago when I was walking along in New York City, looking up at the tall buildings and apartment houses. I came to an empty lot, and there was a group of young boys playing baseball. They had a plank for a bat and a ball that was wrapped with tape.

"I sat down and watched this game for a little while, and I noticed over on the sidelines there was a boy sitting on some rocks, and his legs were dangling. I went over and sat down by this boy and learned he had fallen on the ice and was paralyzed from his waist down. I talked with him a little more and found out there was an operation that could be performed, but it was very costly and the boy's parents didn't have the necessary funds.

"I went back to my hotel room, and I sat down and I wrote some letters, and it wasn't very long before I started receiving replies. Checks and one-hundred-dollar bills came out of those envelopes, and soon I had the money. I went back to the boy and with the aid of his parents made the necessary arrangements with the doctor."

The speaker paused, then added, "Gentlemen, ten years have passed since that day, and I'm very happy to say that the operation was successful. The boy could walk as though he had never been injured. And I wish I could say that this boy is now himself a very successful doctor or lawyer or businessman or athlete. But as I stand here today, the tears in my eyes are because I have just received word that this boy is in prison, waiting to be executed. It simply proves once again that men and dollars can provide the means of performing an operation that can make a boy walk, but that only God can guide a boy's footsteps."

And I'm excited about the Fellowship of Christian Athletes because of an experience that took place in my own life seven years ago. I was invited to come and take part in a city-wide meeting in Columbia, South Carolina. I was asked to be on the stage with eleven athletes. And Mr. President, I sat on that end chair scared to death, because I knew that a little later they were going to call on me to speak for five minutes.

I watched as notable men in the field of sports stood up and stated without embarrassment what Jesus Christ meant to them. I looked out in the audience and there were six to eight hundred people sitting there on a Sunday afternoon, but I was still thinking about my time before that microphone. And then big Bill Glass, who was then defensive end for the Cleveland Browns, stood—all six-five, two-hundred-sixty-five pounds—and he grabbed that microphone, and he quoted a verse of Scripture that I was not too familiar with. It's found in Romans, the First Chapter, the 16th verse, and it says: "For I am not ashamed of the Gospel of Christ: for it is the power of God unto salvation to every one that believeth." And I remember thinking that here is a man that is unashamed, but, more than that, he's glad to stand up and to share what is very real in his life.

Later, we divided up into pairs, and Bill and I got together, went into a couple of civic clubs and high school assemblies—and then out to the state penitentiary. I remember that as we walked I saw a boy that I knew, a boy that was having to pay for his misdeeds with time out of his life. We walked into a chapel that was filled to capacity—sort of like it is here today, except they were required to go. And big Bill Glass stood up, and he shared again what Jesus Christ meant to him.

I'll never forget that as we walked out after the service one of the younger inmates reached out and grabbed us by our arms. He asked very simply, "Why is it that I hear about Jesus Christ now, in here, for the very first time in my life?"

And this is the reason that I am excited about a national organization of Christian athletes who have banded together with the express purpose of challenging athletes and, through them, the youth of the nation, with the adventure of following Christ in the fellowship of the Church.

My wife and I flew up to Washington yesterday morning, because I was so nervous I felt I needed some time in a room alone to prepare. And we just happened to come up on a plane that was loaded with South Carolina rooters, going to the game with Maryland. Some of you probably know how the game came out. Our boys didn't win; they lost. Maryland hadn't won a game, but they beat South Carolina yesterday.

My wife and I didn't sit together on the plane, because we were a little late getting on. My wife sat over there, and I was over here, and she struck up a conversation with a very fine-looking gentleman from South Carolina. In the course of the conversation, he mentioned that he and his wife never flew together on the same plane. "We don't want to go down together," he explained.

My wife followed up this statement by asking him, "If this plane goes down, do you know where you'll go?" Well, he paused for a moment or two and then he gave her, halfheartedly, a good-works type answer. And then, from the Bible, she shared with him how he might know where he's going if that plane just happened to go down. He thought about it for a little bit but didn't respond.

What I'd like to do for the next several minutes is to ask you to think about a text that would answer this abiding question of mankind: How might I win eternal life? I'd like, first of all, to read a passage of Scripture that's found in Mark, the 10th Chapter. Here we talk about a young man who asks this abiding question: How might I inherit eternal life? And then the answer is given. Starting with the 17th verse, where Jesus is walking along, we read: "And when he was gone forth into the way, there came one running, and kneeled to him, and asked him, Good Master, what shall I do to inherit eternal life? And Jesus said unto him, Why callest thou me good? there is none good but one, that is, God. Thou knowest the commandments, Do not commit adultery, Do not kill, Do not steal, Do not bear false witness, Defraud not, Honour thy father and mother. And he answered and said unto them, Master, all these have I observed from my youth. Then Jesus beholding him loved him, and said unto him, One thing thou lackest: go thy way, sell whatsoever thou hast, and give to the poor, and thou shalt have treasure in heaven: and come, take up the cross, and follow me. And he was sad at that saying, and went away grieved: for he had great possessions."

Now, first of all, I sense that this was an athlete, because you notice he came *running* up to Jesus. He had the right attitude. Number two, he asked the right question: How might I inherit or win eternal life? This truly is the abiding question of mankind. Number three, he asked the right person. He didn't go to India and ask a guru. He didn't get caught up in the surrealism that characterizes our younger generation. He went to God's Son, Jesus Christ, the Messiah, with his question.

And number four, he got the right answer. Jesus looked at him and he loved him and he said sell what you have and give to the poor and come and follow me. This is the same Jesus Christ who said, "I am the way, the truth, and the life: no man cometh unto the Father but by me." Number five, he made the wrong decision. He turned and put his head down and he walked away. He had had his moment with Jesus, but there was something in his life that kept him from making this commitment. It might be power; it might be prestige; it might be money; it could be almost anything.

I had my moment with Jesus when I was a teenager. The pastor of my church came around to my home one day and sat down, and I didn't want to be there. I remember so well that I wanted to be outside playing baseball, but I was cornered in there for a little bit, and the minister said some things that changed my life.

He used the verse where Jesus said, "I am the way, the truth, and the *life*." Then he started talking about sin and I knew he had me there. He followed with the penalty of sin: "The wages of sin is death." But then he came by with the good news: "Christ died for our sins . . . ; he was buried, and . . . he rose again the third day according to the scriptures." That day, as a teenager, I responded and accepted Jesus Christ as Lord and Saviour of my life.

I'm not about to stand up here today and say that I've had a victorious life all these years. There's been defeat in my life. There have been many times when I've turned from His way and gone my way; I wanted to coach and run my own life.

But just recently I've had an experience that made me again turn my life over to the Person of Jesus Christ, and how grateful I am for that. So many times I've stood up in front of a group like this, and I've said something like this: "Our culture today needs real men, men with inner poise who offer stubborn resistance against the flaunting of moral laxity, irreligion, loose living, luxury-loving, comfort-seeking drunkenness that is saturating and destroying our society." I've said further that we need a man who dares to stand for a principle, dares to uphold the right against all odds, doesn't yield easily to the whims of the crowd, dares not to laugh at obscene stories, is indignant when men use the name of Christ in cursing, smear it around with filthy banners and lewd jokes; one who has the courage to guard what is sacred and dares to profess love for God in the midst of a materialistic secular crowd that might jeer.

But you know, as I've said these things, it wasn't true in my life, and I knew that I was a hypocrite as I was saying these words.

I was so grateful just a little bit ago when the President and all of us were having coffee outside, and Rex Kern came up to me and he said, "What Scripture would you like for me to use today?" And I said, "Rex, did you have any in mind?" and he said the First Chapter of First John, and then he read the very passage of Scripture that's meant so much in my life just recently. The 7th verse says, "But if we walk in the light, as he is in the light, we have fellowship one with another, and the blood of Jesus Christ his Son cleanseth us from all sin."

I'd like to close with an illustration, because as far as the world goes, there are so many of us who apparently have won and are leading the victorious life. The title of what I really want to say today is "To Win and Yet Lose." But when my wife mentioned this to Jim Jeffrey, he looked up and said, you've got it backwards —you mean to lose and then win." But as far as the world is concerned, there are so many of us that seemingly are winning, yet when death comes around perhaps all is lost.

And I would like to tell you the story of a doctor—a very wealthy man who found his son in an army hospital. He was delighted to see that his son was recovering and would have no permanent scars or handicaps. As the two of them talked, the young man said, "That must be Jim's dad over there." The boy's eyes had wandered from his father's face to a nearby bed, where a horribly broken body lay in awful misery, and a quiet, ordinary-looking man stood at his side. "Who is Jim?" asked the father. The son replied, "A fellow from our outfit; he's dying; swell kid."

The man of affluence looked at the drama of life and death being enacted so close to him. Nurses and doctors were there. It was obvious that death was near. He was startled to see the father of the dying soldier move down to the foot of the bed and start singing. It didn't sound like a choir. It was feeble, it was broken in spots, but it was singing. And he could only ask, "How could you sing like that?"

The man looked up and replied, "I have missed much that most men count valuable. I have lost a farm. I have failed at business. I have very little worldly goods, but one thing I made sure of—I led my boy to Jesus. Now I shall lose my boy but not forever. Some men gain a great deal and lose it all at death. I have lost a great deal, but I shall gain far more when I step into heaven."

Finally, I'd like to say very simply that so far as my own life is concerned, anything good, anything that seemingly has brought lasting peace and joy into my life, I recognize as a gift which has come to me through Jesus Christ my Saviour. I think I could sum up the Fellowship of Christian Athletes and my remarks today by some words that were written by a fellow who never played one game of athletics in his life. His name is Walt Huntley, and he put together some words and entitled his little composition "God's Hall of Fame." The ultimate in each one of our lives here today is heaven. In baseball, the ultimate is the Hall of Fame. And Huntley's words are these:

> Your name may not appear down here
>     In this world's hall of fame,
> In fact, you may be so unknown
>     That no one knows your name;
> The Oscars and the praise of men
>     May never come your way,
> But don't forget God has rewards
>     That He'll hand out someday.
>
> This hall of fame is only good
>     As long as time shall be;
> But keep in mind, God's Hall of Fame
>     Is for eternity;
> To have your name inscribed up there
>     Is greater more by far
> Than all the fame and all the praise
>     Of every man-made star.
>
> This crowd on earth, they soon forget
>     When you're not at the top.
> They'll cheer like mad until you fall,

And then their praise will stop;
Not God, He never does forget,
And in His Hall of Fame,
By just believing on His Son,
Forever there's your name.

I'll tell you, friend, I wouldn't trade
My name, however small,
That's written there beyond the stars
In that celestial Hall,
For all the famous names on earth,
Or glory that they share;
I'd rather be an unknown here,
And have my name up there.

Thank you.

MR. WILKINSON: Lord, we are grateful for the opportunity to worship together in fellowship in this house. We remember prayerfully this morning all those involved in the Fellowship of Christian Athletes and also all those concerned with the responsibility for the government of our nation and all nations of the world. Grant that the words that we have said and sung with our lips and heard with our ears, we may also believe in our hearts and practice and show forth in our lives. And may your blessing be upon us all, both now and forevermore. Amen.

*November 22, 1970*

Prelude

Opening Remarks                    THE PRESIDENT

Doxology

Prayer                    THE RIGHT REVEREND MONSIGNOR
                                THOMAS J. McCARTHY
                          Pastor, St. John Fisher Parish
                          Palos Verdes Peninsula, California

Anthem                    THE HOPE COLLEGE CHAPEL CHOIR
                                    Holland, Michigan
                          *"Prayer for Peace"* by Paul Fetler

Sermon                    *"Now Thank We All Our God—*
                          *A Thanksgiving Meditation"*

Anthem          THE HOPE COLLEGE CHAPEL CHOIR
          *"O, Clap Your Hands"* by Ralph Vaughan Williams

Benediction

Postlude

# The Right Reverend Monsignor
# Thomas J. McCarthy

THE PRESIDENT: Mrs. Nixon and I want to welcome this very distinguished company of guests to the White House Worship Service this morning—and also to welcome those who will be participating in the service.

We have a splended musical organization for our service today, the Hope College Chapel Choir from Holland, Michigan. During its eighteen years as a touring concert group, the choir has appeared in twenty-five states, Canada, and seven European countries. It has been the guest choir six times at the Easterdawn Service in Radio City Music Hall—the only choir to appear more than once at this event. Under the direction of Dr. Robert Cavanaugh, the Hope College Chapel Choir has gained the reputation of being perhaps one of the four or five outstanding musical organizations of its kind in the college and universities of this nation. This house is most honored to have these young people with us today.

In welcoming Monsignor McCarthy, we welcome him first as a member of the press. He has a distinguished record in that respect. He was formerly editor of *The Tidings*, the outstanding publication of the Archdiocese of Los Angeles. Later he was located for several years here, in Washington, where he headed the public information program of the Catholic Bishops. He also served as the Catholic representative, in a public information capacity, for the programs of the Voice of America, and in this

203

work he has appeared a number of times on television and radio. The Monsignor is now pastor of St. John Fisher Parish, located on the Palos Verdes Peninsula in California.

We are honored to have Monsignor McCarthy here today, not only as a distinguished member of the clergy, but as a friend of more than twenty-five years. We are greatly pleased that he will conduct our Worship Service this morning.

MONSIGNOR McCARTHY: O God, our help in ages past, our hope in years to come, receive this tribute of our worship and hear our prayer as we assemble this morning and offer thee our praise and thanksgiving. Thou hast richly fulfilled our founding fathers' faith in thy providence by giving us a land rich in the abundance of thy creation. Let us not be prodigal in the use of thy gifts, but be ever mindful of our obligation to share them generously with those who are less advantaged than we.

Freedom, justice, and brotherhood by thy grace have become for us a precious reality. But for countless men all over the world, they are still but a dream. May we be faithful in sharing our heritage with the living and transmit it intact to all who are yet unborn.

We ask a special blessing upon him who is our President, to whom as a people we have entrusted the guidance and direction of our nation in this time of stress and test. Give him the light to lead us on, the courage of heart to bear his burdens manfully, and the wisdom and knowledge to know thy will in all regards.

Bless her who is his companion, his strength, our First Lady, and his family.

Bless our Congress and our courts and all who give their strength, their knowledge, and their lives to the service of our country. Let their dedication and example inspire us. We ask this in thy name, O Lord.

At this nostalgic time of year, when the harvest has been gathered and stored, when the leaves have shed their autumnal glory and fallen to the ground, when a bracing tang sharpens the early morning air, and the days grow short and the dusk falls early, it long has seemed good to our people to pause in their busy round and join in public thanksgiving to their Creator for His generous bounty and for His provident care in bringing them safely, by a way they did not know, to the end of another year.

What we do on our national day of Thanksgiving constitutes the noblest and best action we are capable of, as a people. For, in that action, we raise our minds and hearts in prayer and gratefully proclaim: Now thank we all our God—for the blessings that have been our common lot; for the creature comforts that have placed our nation among the favored regions of the earth; for the fruitful yield of the soil which has fed us; for the richer yield from labor of every kind which has sustained our lives; for all those gifts to man which have quickened his faith in his manhood, and have nourished and strengthened his spirit to do the great work before him; for that honor which is held above price; and for that courage and zeal which stimulate his quest for truth, no matter the cost; surely, so rich a bounty is worthy of our grateful acknowledgment.

It is a happy circumstance, then, that finds us gathered here, on this first day of that week in which we celebrate our national day of Thanksgiving. What we do here, accords fittingly with what our people, by Presidential proclamation, are encouraged to do on next Thursday—to thank and to praise Him from whom all blessings flow. It is a particular joy to share with him, who is our President, and with his and our gracious First Lady, this worship service in which we express thanks to God for past favors and beg His continued guidance for our beloved nation in the days ahead.

What shall we say of those days? What will they be like? Not easy ones! Not without their burdens of anxiety, their stern challenges, and trials by fire! They will be a time of *testing*, to be sure! But we cannot be unnerved by that prospect any more than we can succumb to that sense of futility which the prophets of doom indulge, today, because of so many fears at large, so many ancient certainties and loyalties questioned and so many decent hopes shattered. A people whose proud affirmation proclaims them as a *nation under God* must find it within their spiritual resources to quicken their faith and to deepen their trust in Him, when their national character is tested.

Now the test of any good sailor is never taken in calm waters. It is best taken in heavy weather, when winds are contrary, the sea is rising, and the elements batter at him from every side. Wise is he, in that time of testing, if he heeds the poet's assurance:

> Say not the struggle naught availeth,
>   The labor and the wounds are vain,
> The enemy faints not, nor faileth,
>   And as things have been, they remain.
>
> If hopes were dupes, fears may be liars;
>   It may be, in yon smoke conceal'd,
> Your comrades chase e'en now the fliers,
>   And, *but for you*, possess the field.
>
> For while the tired waves, vainly breaking,
>   Seem here no painful inch to gain,
> Far back, through creeks and inlets making,
>   Comes silent, flooding in, the main.

Let us remember that! Let us take heart from those deep reserves in the American character which have always had their source "far back, through creeks and inlets making" and which, unfailingly, have "come silent, flooding in," carrying us on their surging crest to that high eminence we hold now, as a nation and as a people. Such reserves give a richer promise for our future and a greater cause for thanksgiving than all the tired negations so noisily bruited about today, by that element in our society which is forever disparaging its origins and denigrating its past, all the while it arrogantly claims that the future belongs to it.

The future belongs to no man, to no group of men. It belongs to God. All that we, His creatures, are vouchsafed is a knowledge of the present *only* and *whatever* we can retain of the remembered past. That, however, is enough for our needs. It enables us to assess our age with the words Dickens used to describe the age of the French Revolution: "It was the best of times, it was the worst of times."

Taking the negative aspect first, it is the worst of times because two destructive factors have been at work within our civilization which have altered it substantially from that civilization which our fathers knew. These two factors are first, the abandonment on a widespread scale of a practical belief in the divine, supernatural order, and second, the shocking moral collapse which has followed that abandonment of belief.

The world of our fathers took for granted the existence of a higher world than this daily one of which we have direct experience. Any denial of that world would have been to them a spiritual and intellectual shock. They never pridefully assumed that they were the measure of all things, nor did they act as though they were. They were too wise for that! Instead, they saw all life as it related to God. The goodness or badness of a life was determined by its conformity or lack of conformity to His standards. Into the greatest of their political documents they incorporated their openly professed belief that all men are created equal, that they are endowed by their Creator with inalienable rights, and that they are inalienable because they have their roots in God. This steady and sturdy recognition of God's central and crucial place in the affairs of men, to which our fathers gave their assent, has been denied and abandoned in large segments of American society today, and all of us are the poorer for it. The basic fact of man's existence is that he was *made by* and is *meant for* God. If he chooses to ignore that, he must be prepared to pay a dear price for his rashness.

Some measure of the dear price he is paying is tragically borne in upon us as we look at the current moral wreckage in our

society: the broken homes with the traumatic effects they have
had upon our children; the widespread addiction to drugs and
alcohol; the ever-widening incidence of homosexuality and lesbi-
anism with their strident bid for social acceptance; the complete
breakdown of authority all the way down the line; the veritable
tidal wave of pornographic garbage which poses as literature and
not only corrupts good tast but offends elemental decency; the
sick humor which infects the most sacred precincts of life and
makes vile all that comes within its scatalogical touch; the mind-
less, irrational violence that issues from the anarchic ranks of our
alienated youth, so hell-bent on destruction, but with no decent
alternatives to replace what they so wantonly destroy.

Such is the witches' bitter brew which stirs and boils before our
eyes! It is not a pretty picture, surely; but it is made less pretty
by twentieth-century man's inability to grasp how much of that
bitterness has its source in his foolish pretension that he can play
God and usurp His role in the governance of man. Until he can
recapture and accept that ancient bit of wisdom which reminds
us that while man proposes, it is ultimately God who disposes, he
must accept the responsibility for the parlous state in which our
present society finds itself. The pollution of his *natural* resources
—the air he breathes, the water he drinks, the plants he sprays,
the seas, lakes, and rivers he befouls with his wastes—what are
these against the spiritual resources he has squandered in his
foolish attempt to make life here on this earth serve only his mean
and selfish purposes without any provision for God's gifts and
God's will in his regard?

A naïve belief in science, to the exclusion of any belief in God,
cannot save him from folly, no matter how much he may trust in
its power to open new dimensions for his humanity in outer
space. It is within *here*—not out *there*—that he will find the source
of his real growth and peace. His true frontier is *inner* man, not
*outer* space; and only at that frontier will he discover the rich
meaning and purpose of his human existence, which so largely

escapes him now, but which his fathers, before him, knew so well. Their hard-earned wisdom, distilled from past experience, still has much to say to our human condition today.

From the tub-sitting and the shadow-measuring of the ancient Greeks to our eye-popping modern cyclotrons and moonshots has been a fabulous, spectacular range of technological achievement. But the prophets of old still speak to our human needs with more immediacy than the latest bulletins from Houston or Cape Kennedy; and our cherished and ancient Judaeo-Christian heritage challenges us to far greater heights than any achieved by our astronauts.

More and more Americans are realizing this and it is because of that encouraging fact that we can say of our age, "It is the best of times." We are not as spiritually sterile, as completely hobbled by fear and hopelessness over our prospects as certain signs and portents would indicate. Not all the flags that fly in this time of test are distress signals. Many of them lift the heart with their proclamation of a new life, a new day, a new spiritual vigor, for which we give fervent thanks. Just as in the collapse of the Roman Empire fifteen centuries ago a discerning man might have seen forces at work which would survive the wreck of an empire, and not only survive but help to fashion a new world as well, so, too, it is possible today to discern stirrings of the spirit which, if properly recognized, can give shape and substance to that kind of world which each of us in his heart longs for so earnestly.

There is the searching examination, for instance, which all our institutions—church, state, school, and family—are undergoing, at present, with the insistent demand that they must earn anew the respect of the "now generation" by abandoning their "business as usual" approach and revealing their openness, their relevance, and their sense of commitment to the solution of the burning questions of our day.

There is an intense personalism, particularly in our young, manifesting itself in vital concerns with their environment, the uses and abuses of it; with the deep sense of personal importance that every human being has, regardless of color; with the legal guarantees of the civil rights of each individual and their implementation in practice; with the ministry of service to the needs of the alienated and the lonely in our society; with the problems posed by injustice, discrimination, consumer fraud, political chicanery and venality in public office; with the horror and havoc wreaked by war on human life and human resources; with the need for schools to come to grips with the "gut" issues of our day and to move out from the ivory tower into the hurly-burly of modern life where problems are seen not in abstraction but in terms of human faces manifesting hunger, anger, and frustration; and, finally, with all those issues involving life, liberty, and the pursuit of happiness, which, for too long, have remained bracketed under the unfinished business of government but which can no longer be pidgeonholed or allowed to die in committee.

We have moved out, thank God, from the precincts of organized charity and compassion where the cry of the poor has been screened from our ears and the stench of their poverty has never reached our nostrils. We should be encouraged by those attempts which are being made by government and by public and private agencies of welfare to redress the imbalances of an economy which tolerates the polarization of the "haves" and the "have nots." We should be heartened by the growing public insistence that the medical care of the poor and the disadvantaged members of our society be equal to their medical needs. The American conscience has given abundant evidence that it has been touched by the moral quality of these pressing concerns and that it will not be satisfied until they are effectively dealt with. For this, we must be grateful.

This is no time to don the widow's weeds and to weep over our failures in the past. We are a people of hope! We are a people to whom the future beckons; and men of spiritual vision and men of hope are always given deeper vision than those whose eyes are held fast by material concerns only. It is because of that depth of vision that is granted to us as a people that we can cry out this triumphant affirmation:

> "Ye that have faith to look with fearless eyes
> Beyond the tragedy of a world at strife:
> And know that out of death and night,
> Shall rise the dawn of ampler life.
> Rejoice, (whatever anguish rend the heart,)
> That God has given you the priceless dower
> To live in these great times, and play your
> Part in freedom's crowning hour.
> That ye may tell your sons who see the light
> High in the heavens—their heritage to take—
> "I saw the powers of darkness take their flight:
> I saw the morning break."
>
>                                   (Owen Seamen)

Please God, we will live to see that promise fulfilled for our children!

Oh, Almighty God, Father of all of us and Lord of the universe, all good things have issued from thy hands, and thou hast made us stewards of thy rich gifts and blessings. Let us not forget thee.

> The tumult and the shouting dies;
> The captains and the kings depart:
> But still stands Thine ancient sacrifice,
> An humble and a contrite heart.

> Lord God of Hosts,
> Be with us yet,
> Lest we forget!
> Lest we forget!

*October 10, 1971*

| | |
|---|---|
| Prelude | |
| Opening Remarks | THE PRESIDENT |
| Prayer | DR. D. ELTON TRUEBLOOD<br>Professor at Large, Earlham College<br>Richmond, Indiana |
| Doxology | |
| Scriptural Reading | CLIFFORD M. HARDIN<br>Secretary of Agriculture |
| Anthem | |
| Sermon | |
| Anthem | |
| Benediction | |
| Postlude | |

# Dr. D. Elton Trueblood

THE PRESIDENT: Mr. Chief Justice, Members of the Cabinet, Members of the Diplomatic Corps, Members of the Congress, and all of our special guests this morning: For these worship services this is a rather unusual one. Those of you who have attended before recognize that all of them have been ecumenical in the broadest sense. We have had representatives of many of the major Protestant groups, Catholic groups, and Hebrew groups. But very seldom has the denomination of which I am a member been represented.

This morning Dr. Elton Trueblood, one of the great scholars of the Society of Friends and now Professor at Large of Earlham College, who is well known to many of you in this room, will bring the message. And the Secretary of Agriculture, whose parents, just as my parents, were birthright Quakers, will read the Scripture.

DR. TRUEBLOOD: We thank thee O Father for this day, this place, and this nation. We thank thee for the faith which unites us and for the power which sustains us. We come together in simplicity, in quietness, and in humility, praying that we may know thy will and that we may have the courage to follow it. We pray especially this morning for the President of this great nation, for the members of Congress, the Supreme Court, and the Cabinet and all who make decisions in the life of this people. Help them to know that they are under thee. Help them to be instruments of thy divine will. All this we ask for the sake of Jesus Christ our Lord. Amen.

One hundred and nine years ago at this time of year there was a meeting for worship in this building. It was in the darkest period of the Civil War, when President Lincoln met with a group of people in a time of worship of almighty God. He was facing some of the most difficult decisions which ever came in his entire career. It was in October 1862. This has constantly been in my mind since President Nixon graciously invited me to lead the worship this morning.

Human beings are people who make decisions and who live by decisions. In this we differ from all other creatures on earth. The decisions made by some people in this room make a great deal of difference in the lives of other people. But how are decisions to be made? There are no simple answers. There are no ready-made answers.

All of us as very young people studied algebra, and we remember that there was always the possibility of turning to the back of the book and there would be an answer. But life isn't like that; there are none such. We have to struggle to find them! What we all know is that the answers come not by a slide rule, but because of the richness of our resources. Every human being draws constantly upon the whole background of his life.

This is why I've asked Secretary Hardin to read the Scripture that he has read. It is, as you know, the best known of all the parables of Christ—the Parable of the Seeds and the Sower. There are two very striking things that you may notice about this parable. First, all have the same seed, but there is a tremendous difference in the productivity. Some produce nothing while others produce thirtyfold, and sixtyfold, one-hundredfold. The spectrum of human productivity is very, very wide. But what is even more striking is the account given in the last words that Clifford Hardin read: that because they have no depth of root they wither away.

Now, here is our problem as individuals and as a nation. How can we have the depth of roots which will make our actions less likely to be wrong? Here we may profit enormously by the pattern of Christ who is indeed our Pattern.

As I read the Gospels, I am continually impressed by the fact that Christ was always drawing on a large deposit of spiritual resources, most of these coming from the Hebrew Scriptures. For example, when he went back to his home town of Nazareth and he had an opportunity to state the whole theme of his operation, they gave him the book. He could have opened it anywhere. He opened, actually, to the 61st Chapter of Isiah, and this is what he read: "The Spirit of the Lord is upon me. He hath anointed me to preach deliverance to the captives, to set free those that are bound." He was telling that his whole operation was Operation Liberation. But he did not invent it; He drew, instead, on a rich resource.

Think also of Christ on the cross. We know that the words that he used on the cross come mostly from the Psalms. The very last words that he uttered were from the 31st Psalm: "Father, into thy hands I commit my spirit."

When I turn to Psalm 31 these words move me tremendously. We do not know how Christ looked. We don't know whether he was tall or short. We don't know anything about his features, but we know what he knew so well that he could repeat it without the text in front of him. When I read Psalm 31 I am as close to him as I shall ever be. Perhaps you'd like to hear these words that he clearly knew by heart.

"In thee, O Lord, do I put my trust; let me never be ashamed: deliver me in they righteousness. Bow down thine ear to me; deliver me speedily: be thou my strong rock, for an house of defense to save me. For thou art my rock and my fortress; therefore for thy name's sake lead me, and guide me." This was essentially the prayer that President Lincoln was praying over and over in this building. He was asking for the guiding hand of God.

You will not have exactly these same resources. No two people have exactly the same. But we must have resources of some kind.

Our lives are not easy; our decisions are difficult. Therefore, our task is to build up as much of this depth of root as we can get. If you forget all that I say, remember these words of Christ: "Because they have no depth of root, they withered away."

We have tried the experiment of keeping alive wonderful things such as equality of opportunity and the dignity of the individual, but often they have been severed from their sustaining roots and in this we cannot win. However beautiful the flowers may be, if they are cut from their roots, they will wither and die. This is why it is a wonderful thing that in the most famous building of America, people should gather quietly to worship almighty God.

Now go in joy, sin no more, love God, serve His children. Amen.